CRYSTALS BEGINNER'S GUIDE TO CRYSTAL HEALING

How to Heal the Human Energy Field Through the Power of Crystals and Healing Stones

Crystal Lee

TABLE OF CONTENTS

Introduction 2
Chapter 1 *What Are Crystals?* 4
Chapter 2 *Crystal Energy – Where Does It Come From?* 12
Chapter 3 *Benefits Of Healing With Crystals* 18
Chapter 4 *Crystals And Chakras* 27
Chapter 5 *Crystal Grids* 34
Chapter 6 *Why You Should Learn/Practice Crystal Healing* 47
Chapter 7 *Healing Fundamentals* 53
Chapter 8 *How To Choose The Right Crystals* 64
Chapter 9 *Crystals And What Ails You* 72
Chapter 10 *What Crystal For What?* 93
Conclusion 108
Description 109

© Copyright 2018 by Crystal Lee - All rights reserved.

The following eBook is reproduced below with the goal of providing information that is as accurate and reliable as possible. Regardless, purchasing this eBook can be seen as consent to the fact that both the publisher and the author of this book are in no way experts on the topics discussed within and that any recommendations or suggestions that are made herein are for entertainment purposes only. Professionals should be consulted as needed prior to undertaking any of the action endorsed herein.

This declaration is deemed fair and valid by both the American Bar Association and the Committee of Publishers Association and is legally binding throughout the United States.

Furthermore, the transmission, duplication, or reproduction of any of the following work including specific information will be considered an illegal act irrespective of if it is done electronically or in print. This extends to creating a secondary or tertiary copy of the work or a recorded copy and is only allowed with the express written consent from the Publisher. All additional right reserved.

The information in the following pages is broadly considered a truthful and accurate account of facts and as such, any inattention, use, or misuse of the information in question by the reader will render any resulting actions solely under their purview. There are no scenarios in which the publisher or the original author of this work can be in any fashion deemed liable for any hardship or damages that may befall them after undertaking information described herein.

Additionally, the information in the following pages is intended only for informational purposes and should thus be thought of as universal. As befitting its nature, it is presented without assurance regarding its prolonged validity or interim quality. Trademarks that are mentioned are done without written consent and can in no way be considered an endorsement from the trademark holder.

INTRODUCTION

For thousands of years, crystals have become a significant part of healing. Whether it is for emotional, mental, or physical recovery, people have recognized the power hidden inside these beautiful gems. But for a time, the practice was relegated to the mysteries of the dark spirits. It was something that was tantamount to striking a deal with the devil to even be seen using crystals and for that reason, for a number of generations, the practice of crystal healing was looked down upon.

But today, in our modern world of technology, this art is experiencing a rebirth. No one can deny any longer the vibrations hidden inside each of these ancient stones and the power that they have over many people. Their ability to channel both the emotional and spiritual energy they possess and direct it to areas where it can cause true positive change is starting to be accepted again.

Every day, crystals are being used in a variety of ways from making a connection to your inner spiritual being to helping people through their emotional struggles. They have found a new life again.

Many who are unfamiliar with crystals, fail to realize that we are not just physical beings. There is a very powerful connection between every element that exists inside all of us. Crystals are simply a tool that can be used to connect all the different parts of our beings (the physical, mental, emotional, and spiritual) together, and as it does, it can have a powerful effect on every aspect of our lives.

The problem is that few understand when these elements of our whole being are out of balance, things can go terribly wrong. We tend to spend too much time dwelling with our mental thoughts, to the point of losing touch with the rest of who we are. As a result of this imbalance, we struggle with illnesses, depression, and even struggle physically. We find ourselves lost and alone in a world full of people. Relationships begin to suffer, we lose our jobs, and we fail to achieve our true purpose in life.

Today's world, full of all the modern conveniences we can imagine, places a lot of stress on the mental and physical bodies. Nearly everything we do is out of balance. Our lives are hectic and as a result, we make sacrifices of the things we know, deep down, that we should hold dear to us. It starts with little things but in time, it builds up to those big things that we can no longer ignore. In the end, we walk around like empty shells unable to find joy in anything. And if the problem is left unaddressed for too long, it will start to affect us physically. That's usually the time when we start to realize something has gone wrong, but in our innocence of the deeper things of life, we are unable to really identify it.

The answer may not be as aloof as you think. Turning to crystals to help you find yourself, regain mastery over your own life, and heal the inner person may be the very thing you've been searching for. In this book, we will guide you to understand how crystals can work and the benefits you can gain from them. You'll learn…

- What crystals really are and the power they possess
- The source of its energy
- The history of crystal healing
- How you can benefit from using crystals to heal
- What are chakras and how crystals can help you connect to them
- Why you need crystal grids and how to create one
- Why everyone should learn something about crystals
- How to use crystals to heal what ails you
- And so much more

You can consider this book your guide to a whole new world. One that puts the power of your life back into your hands. You can use it like a map that will lead you to a bigger, better, happier, and healthier self that you won't ever want to neglect again.

CHAPTER 1
What Are Crystals?

We'll start our journey by coming to understand what crystals are from a scientific perspective. To the average person, a crystal is nothing more than a pretty rock. Likely that makes you wonder just how an inanimate object like a rock is going to help you heal. This is a normal reaction by most people and is probably one of the main reasons why so many are reluctant to recognize the healing powers hidden inside each one of these precious gems.

Yes, it is true that crystals are on the surface just another type of stone, but each one is unique and you won't find any other stone with the kind of properties it possesses. Every crystal has its own energetic properties that can be channeled in all sorts of directions. These beautiful rock formations can be used in thousands of different ways, many of which go far beyond mere decoration.

This is not just some spiritistic hype that only those with blind faith might believe. Few people realize that the world's first radios were only able to transmit their signals with the aid of crystals. It is a scientific fact that we will discuss throughout the following pages of this book. While people see first their natural beauty and want to put them in the same company as they would diamonds and rubies, looking beyond the surface will reveal so much more.

What are Crystals and Where Do They Come From

In scientific terms, crystals are simply a grouping of molecules and atoms. While they are hardened like a stone, each crystal has its own unique characteristics. First, they are formed from a variety of different natural materials on earth. Some are made from salt, and others come from other elements found in the natural world. Gemologists and geologists have a unique definition of a crystal. They describe it as a solid object with atoms that are organized in a repeating lattice pattern. While there are several different crystal patterns, we're only going to focus on those that can be used for healing. These are sometimes described as gemstones, minerals, or rocks.

Minerals: Not all minerals can be classified as crystals, but those that are, have a highly organized structure that is formed by the special way the atoms interlock together. As they grow, the variations of temperature and chemical composition that occurs underneath the crust of the earth throughout the eons of time, it takes for them to form to give them their distinctive properties.

Rocks: Rocks are stones that have been formed from several different minerals, but all rocks can be considered as crystals.

Gemstones: These are those rocks that have been cut and polished so that they are more attractive to the human eye. There are two classifications of gemstones — precious, such as diamonds or rubies, and semiprecious such as garnets and quartz.

They come in all shapes and sizes, each having its own set of unique characteristics. The base material the crystal emerges from determines how it will be formed. For example, crystals made from salt will form cube-like shapes, while snowflakes or ice crystals will form into lattices.

The process they go through when forming is referred to as crystallization. They naturally form in nature all around us. When hot liquid (like magma) cools and then hardens, the molecules in the liquid start to bond together in order to create stability. As they do this, they create a uniform pattern that repeats over and over again until they form a crystal. Other types of crystals are formed when water evaporates from a mixture. This is how salt crystals are created.

You can actually see this with your own eyes. If you want to try a little experiment, take a teaspoon of table salt and put it into regular tap water and let it sit for 24 hours. When you check it again, you will see how the cube crystals have begun to form. These are created because as the water evaporates, the salt atoms are pulled closer together. As more water evaporates, the atoms will continue to pull together until they create a cluster. Eventually, you'll be able to see the cluster with the naked eye in the form of salt crystals.

You will notice that each crystal has its own distinctive shape, which develops based on the type of molecules and atoms at its base. It doesn't matter if the crystal is large or small, if it has the same base molecules and atoms, it will have the same shape.

Of course, not all crystals are formed so quickly, but they are all formed in the same way. Some like salt can be formed in a matter of days, but others, like those that are carbon-based, may take thousands of years to develop.

Natural crystals that have been formed within the earth's crust, often take millions of years to develop. However, today there are many crystals that are now being developed in laboratories. This is because a true crystal is extremely rare to find these days, but if you do have the privilege to own one, you will have in your possession an extremely powerful tool with the ability to do wonderful things.

Many people will sell you crystals, but they are not naturally formed. Natural crystals will always have some type of imperfection that can be spotted if you examine them closely. Those made in the laboratory will be perfect, absent of any flaws. Natural crystals can be dyed a different color or altered in some other way, but a laboratory made crystal can't be changed.

Another important difference is in the cost and the practicality of it. While a man-made crystal will have some level of energy, it will be far less than those that have been carefully made in the bowels of the earth for thousands of years. So, while they may be less expensive, you won't get the same results you get with natural crystals when you use them.

The Power Inside the Crystal

You've probably already experienced the power and vibration in a room without even realizing it. It's that feeling you get when you're in a room full of happy people, everyone smiling, laughing, and enjoying themselves. Then without any explanation, another person enters the room and the entire atmosphere changes. There seems to have been a sudden drain of energy, just by that person's presence.

This is called the Law of Vibration and it shows that everything we see, touch, feel, hear, etc. is made up of energy, even our physical bodies. From the scientific perspective, there is a little difference between you and the furniture in your room. Everything is the product of energy. This energy is constantly in motion, the only difference is that all of it runs on different vibrations. Those that share the same energy and vibrations are considered the same.

As these energies vibrate, we develop thoughts, feelings, emotions, and are spurred on to take different actions, which can have an effect on the vibrations in some form. When we feel down and depressed, our vibrations are low and sluggish, but when we feel up and happy, our vibrations are faster, run at a higher frequency, and produce more energy.

We may not be aware that we emit these types of energies, but as we go about our day, we instinctively respond to those energies that are emanating all around us, and people are also responding to the energy we are putting out. So, if you start your day in a bad mood or on a low vibration, chances are the people around you will respond accordingly. You'll attract the same type of negative energy to you and it will be difficult to move out of that low frequency if you are not aware of it.

The good news is that it doesn't have to be that way. You do have the ability to change it in much the same way as if you wanted to change what you were wearing that day. It all starts with changing the way you think. Once you change your thought process, you'll change your energy. This is the basics of the Law of Attraction. As a result of this change, you will be able to attract a different sort of people to you, those with a faster vibration than what you've normally been pulling in.

It is that energy that exists in all things that has the power to heal whatever it is that ails us. This is not something new or mystic but is at the core of many scientific discoveries. It is the kind of evidence that is used to back up physical theories for more than a century. Albert Einstein's theory of relativity is based on this very knowledge. It is the basis for nuclear power and will be the foundation of many new discoveries to come.

We might be inclined to believe that this energy only exists in living things, but we would be wrong. Even inanimate objects like crystals have their own form of energy and vibrations, and it is when these two connect (humans and crystals) that we begin to see amazing things happen.

Once we understand that all things vibrate, everything starts to become clear. While humans may not be able to automatically sense or identify those vibrations, they are there. In humans, the energy may present itself in three different ways — through chakras, meridians, and auras.

Chakras are the primary energy centers in every human body. Each person has seven different chakras that can be found in specific areas. It can be associated with color and a number of other qualities.

- The first chakra is found at the base of the tailbone
- The second chakra or the sacral is found near the belly button
- The third chakra or the solar plexus sits at the base of the sternum
- The fourth chakra, the heart, sits right in the center of the chest
- The fifth chakra or the throat is found right above the Adam's apple
- The sixth chakra or the third eye sits directly in the center of the forehead
- And the seventh chakra or the crown can be found at the very top of the head

If you could visualize these chakras, you could draw a line directly from the first chakra at the base of the tailbone and draw it in a straight line all the way up through all of the other six, ending at the seventh chakra at the crown of the head.

Meridians are the paths of energy that are running through the body. Auras are the energy fields that are surrounding the body. These auras help us to identify energy in ourselves and in others. They work a little like special cameras for us.

Similar to human bodies, crystals also have their own vibrations and auras, and when the two forms of energy connect, crystal energy can have some sort of effect on our own vibrations. They can be used to help to modify or adjust our energy and as a result, bring about a certain element of healing. In other words, they can change how our energy vibrates.

Now that people are recognizing this internal energy and its effects on the human body, more people are exploring ways to tap into it. Besides through crystals, you might find other treatments once scoffed at becoming increasingly popular. Reflexology and Reiki are just two examples. In the following pages, we're going to show you several ways to use crystals to change your energy and vibrations.

Benefits of Using Crystals

There are many different ways you can benefit from using crystals. Many have found that they help them mentally, emotionally, spiritually, and physically. Some have found practical use when they are used in conjunction with traditional Western style medicine. If they are having a physical problem, they have found that using the crystals will lessen the discomfort they may be feeling or help to relieve the suffering altogether. But aside from easing physical ailments, there are other ways that crystals can be used to your benefit.

- They help you connect to your inner consciousness. They can help you to focus on that inner voice that is constantly running in your head.

- They can assist you psychologically so you can take more positive action in redirecting your life.

- They can clear away any emotional blockages that are getting in your way.

- They help clear away negative energy and thought patterns.

- And they can help you to tap into your more creative side.

We can understand how this is done by understanding the physics of human beings. While we are all made up of vibrating energy, our vibrations are not constant. When we are happy, our vibrations are usually much faster than when we are depressed. Our vibrations change from one day to the next, and even from one situation to another. We're kind of all over the place. When we get close to someone with a low vibration, our vibration usually comes down too. The same is true when we are in the same vicinity as those with a high vibration. We feel good and we pick up on their emotions.

With crystals, it's different. These stones do not have emotions and feelings in the same sense that humans do. Therefore, their vibrations are always constant. They never change, and so they can provide us with a stabilizing effect that is hard for us to achieve on our own.

There are no set rules for how to use crystals. Some people benefit from their energy just by holding them in their hands. Others will keep them close by, in their office, pockets, handbags, etc. Others sleep with them under their pillow or they lie down and place them directly on one of their chakras.

While there are no specific guidelines for how to tap into crystal energy, you do have to have your mind in the right place to gain the most benefit. But when the world is crowding in on you from all sides, it can be difficult to channel your mind in the right direction.

Many who use crystals recommend meditation to help you. This is not something that can be done once in a while. To get the best results, one needs to make a daily practice of meditation for at least 10 to 20 minutes. It will help you to focus long enough to decide on the direction you want to go and what steps you want to take.

This can be a challenge in the beginning, but those who make a habit of it, usually find that in time, they can learn to push out all of their worries and stresses and eventually tap into that inner voice in their head. One of the easiest forms of meditation today is practicing mindfulness. It doesn't require any position to take, nor do you have to worry about chanting any expressions or performing any rituals. Through mindfulness, you simply start to observe your thoughts as a neutral person, looking at them without judgment.

By doing this, you separate yourself from your thoughts and eventually, you will learn to think more clearly. In time, you will feel as though you are a completely separate entity from your thoughts. Then you will be able to connect to your internal energy and channel crystal energy in the right direction.

Other forms of meditation you can adopt are guided imagery, mantra chanting, repetitive movement, and affirmations. Find the type of meditation that works best for you and before long, you'll be able to tap into your energy field and gain the most benefits out of crystal energy.

CHAPTER 2
Crystal Energy – Where Does It Come From?

One of the most common questions asked of beginners is where does the crystal get its energy? Because these gems have been around for thousands of years, there is no real definitive answer to that question. Crystals form in the bowels of the earth, far from human eyes, so much of what we have learned about them is based on a theory first, and then from experience later.

We know that the discovery of their energy happened thousands of years ago, but here is what we have come to learn so far.

Color: You can gauge the energy found in a crystal by its color. When people are drawn to a certain color stone, it is usually the energy that they are attracted to. Different colors have different meanings, which may relate to the elements that form the crystals.

As we learn more about chakras in a later chapter, you'll realize that they too have a deep connection. Crystals help to bring the body's energy into balance through the chakras or the aura. Those crystals that have a combination of different colors also contain additional energy flows and chakras. As you learn more about these energies, you'll begin to understand more about the different colors and what they actually mean.

Shape and Form: Crystals take on all sorts of shapes and sizes. We can learn a lot about the power of crystals from their shape. The concept is related to Sacred Geometry and shapes, similar to the colors of a crystal, will have different meanings associated with them.

For example, crystals with a spiky exterior are more defensive, so they are often selected for protection. Crystals with a round stone are considered to be more feminine, and so are used to ground a person or to bring peace.

But these are not the only considerations when it comes to crystals. You might also look at how the light affects it. If it is transparent, it tends to hold more energy, but if it is reflective, as in a more earthy stone, it is more likely going to be used for grounding.

While many people are not consciously aware of the energy emanating from a crystal, it does exist and it can affect us in many ways. There are some people, however, that tend to be more sensitive to this energy than others. Throughout history, you've probably heard of a long list of those who have been able to not just identify the power of a crystal but have in some ways been able to harness it. Shamans, healers, or those who are believed to possess a unique wisdom or understanding have been able to tap into these stones. Wherever you find yourself lost somewhere on this spectrum, one thing is certain, the power of these crystals cannot be denied, nor can they be ignored. When you are able to connect with this type of energy, you will instinctively know how it will help you.

In today's modern age, we tend to scoff at historical proofs as being primitive and insignificant. It is true, that we live in a fast-paced information age, and with our progressive knowledge of science, we have come to understand much more than our ancestors. Historical records abound that relate to how these gems were used throughout our past.

No doubt, we can learn a lot about the power of these little gems, however, we live in very different times. We cannot rely entirely on historical records to guide us in the proper way to harness crystal energy. Historical documents were often based on superstitions and myths. Today, we can understand the science of these things a lot better. Even now, we are discovering more crystals and minerals every day. We now have scientific evidence of their internal power and have a much better understanding of how to use it. By combining what we have learned from the past with our new understanding, we can use these crystals much more effectively in a lot more ways than we might have otherwise suspected. We can eliminate the mystic superstitions of the past and learn how to use them in a way that will be of benefit to even more people in the world, without fear.

The Power of the Crystal

We've already come to understand that the power of crystals can help with emotional, mental, physical, and spiritual problems. There are a thousand ways to use them in each of these areas. Some people use them exclusively for the treatment of what ails them, while others have found better success in using them in conjunction with other forms of therapy, or as an accompaniment to traditional Western medicine.

You might use it to help with a migraine or you might choose to use them to help with the physical healing of an injury of some type. Some might use them to help put their minds at ease, and still others may use them to help release their creative mind. When it comes to how you use the power of the crystal, the possibilities may be endless.

Enhance Intuition: Like all other creatures, we have a strong instinctive nature. Humans though are naturally intuitive about many things. But in our busy lives, we are often flooded with a myriad of minutia that over time can crowd out your natural intuitiveness. Using crystals to help you bring all of that back, can help you to listen to that inner voice again.

Improve Concentration: It is easy to get distracted in the hectic world we live in. You may find yourself struggling to get out of a rut you've gotten yourself into. Constant distractions can keep you from moving forward. Using crystals along with medication, visualization exercises, and affirmation can make a huge difference.

Break Free from Emotional Baggage: We all carry around suitcases full of emotional baggage. Past traumas and uncomfortable experiences seem to follow us wherever we go. Often, these can get in the way of our ability to move on in our lives. Once you are able to harness the power of crystals, you will clear out much of the baggage that is haunting you and find yourself in a whole new space in your life.

Removing Negative Energy: We've already learned that everything in existence has an energy that influences other things around them. If you find yourself living in a cycle of negative energy, crystals can quickly free your mind and leave you open so more positive forces can find you.

Stimulate Creativity: Our brains are mighty instruments. However, our society has made many of us believe that we don't need to tap into all of our natural resources. We live in a highly analytical world where facts and figures have become more important than creativity. However, when you cannot tap into your creative side, you lose out on many things. Crystals can help you to channel their energy in a way that will allow you to handle your problems in a more creative manner.

Over thousands of years, the power held within crystals has been able to harness the elements found in the earth, the oceans, the sun, the moon, and the stars, and pass them onto us. However, to tap into these powerful resources, you need to come into direct contact with them. However, once you do, you'll find yourself on a journey full of new ways to change your world for the better.

The History of Crystal Healing

The practice of healing crystals has likely been around since the dawn of humanity. While we don't have records that date back that far, we do know that for thousands of years, they have been used for all sorts of things. Many have used them in amulets, as talismans, and other protective ways to ward off evil spirits.

Absence of specific records in recorded history, archaeological digs, and the study of artifacts have revealed how these gems have been used over the years. Here is what we know for sure.

- Approximately 30,000 years ago, amulets were used in what is now part of Great Britain. These were made from Baltic amber, which is located many miles from the location where they were found. This is an indication that for the people of the time to carry them such a long distance, that they were highly valued and likely considered a cherished possession.

- Approximately 12,000 years ago, beads, bracelets, and necklaces were uncovered in several gravesites in the regions of Belgium and Switzerland, indicating that they were likely used to ward off spirits.

- Archaeologists discovered the first recorded use of crystals was in Ancient Sumatra (approximate 1400AD). The records show that the crystals were used in a number of magic formulas, helping us to understand that they recognized the power contained in these stones.

- The Ancient Egyptians used lapis lazuli, carnelian, turquoise, quartz, and emeralds in amulets they wore for their health and protection.

- The Ancient Greeks gave many of the crystals we use today their names. In fact, the word crystal comes from the Greek word for ice. The Greeks actually believed that quartz was water that had been frozen so solidly that it would never thaw again. They wore amethysts as a measure to prevent drunkenness and hangovers, and because of its red color, the name hematite comes from the word blood and was worn by Greek soldiers before a battle in hopes that they would become invincible.

- In Ancient China, jade was the preferred healing stone. Even today, this gem is still very highly valued. Throughout their history, it has been used for kidney ailments and to bring good luck.

- Even during the Renaissance period of history (around 11th century AD), crystal use was combined with herbal remedies to heal all sorts of illnesses.

- During the 1600s, physicians in Germany declared that the power of the gemstone was directly related to the presence of angels, both good and bad.

No doubt there are countless more cases we can find throughout history. While the stones may have received a bad reputation for a time, their rebirth, coupled with modern science, has allowed it to regain its former popularity. Today, however, its use has been adapted to suit our new knowledge of the properties, so we have a much clearer idea of just how to tap into its power and channel that to do even more than anyone else could have possibly done in our history.

CHAPTER 3
Benefits Of Healing With Crystals

It is without question that crystals have these healing powers. Whether we are aware of them or not, the beauty and power of them are widely recognized. You may not be a healer or a shaman, but you too can tap into the power behind these gems and use them in many ways that will benefit you. While we discussed some of the most basic uses for crystals in the last chapter, let's look a little more deeply into what their powers can do here.

Red Crystals

A good example of how color can influence your results is clear by what you can do with red crystals. Long known as a means of activating and energizing, red crystals are associated with your most basic of survival skills. A ruby, one of the most beautiful red crystals, works with the energy of the heart, giving you energy and balance.

Historically, rubies are a representation of royalty and wealth. The color range of rubies can vary from a light pink to a deep red. It is most often connected with the root chakra, but it can also be used to give you the energy you lack. Anyone feeling down or low either emotionally or physically will likely discover that they are losing energy through their aura. Rubies are often used to repair such leaks and to bring more balance to the body so that all energy flows freely.

Red crystals also protect you from psychic attacks, nurture your emotional health, enhance lucid dreaming, stimulates creativity, and gives you spiritual wisdom.

On the other end of the red spectrum, pink crystals can help you to find a resolution to certain problems. It brings emotion and sensitivity to your daily actions. A commonly used crystal, rose quartz, has a very calming effect, but at the same time, it releases many unexpressed emotions that may be buried underneath the surface, inhibiting you from personal growth.

Orange Crystals

Orange crystals work well by combining energizing elements with your ability to focus. This opens the door and allows for more creative skills to emerge. A popular orange crystal is a carnelian, which brings a sense of warmth to its user. It can boost your motivation, stimulate energy, and enhance enthusiasm.

When using carnelian, you will be able to recognize your self-worth, which will naturally help you to heal in a wide range of ways. On a physical level, it can help the body to absorb more vitamins and minerals and ensure that there is enough blood flow to the organs and tissues.

Yellow Crystals

Yellow crystals work well in improving the function of the nervous, digestive, and immune systems. They can ease stress, fear, and anxiety and give you a sense of contentment at the same time. A favorite yellow crystal is an amber, which has been very beneficial in helping the body to heal itself. Citrine quartz, if it is a bright, clear yellow, works well to clear the mind allowing you to focus better. Iron pyrite (sometimes referred to as "fool's gold") cleanses and strengthens the digestive system and leaves you with a sense of calm.

Green Crystals

Green crystals heal the heart, both physically and emotionally. They keep your emotions in balance and move you to build positive relationships. The green aventurine crystal makes it easy for you to express your feelings and can help to relieve anxiety, which will naturally have a positive physical effect as well. Malachite helps you to uncover hidden feelings, so you can break free from unwanted negative behavior patterns. Amazonite heals issues with the throat and the lungs, the bloodstone, and enhances blood circulation to the heart.

Light Blue

Light blue crystals are more often associated with communication and connect to all of the five senses. Its primary focus is on improving the way you talk to yourself. It improves your thought patterns and edifies how you express yourself. The aquamarine crystal promotes better communication, stronger courage, and more confidence. You'll be better able to stand your ground against a formidable foe, and you'll be prepared to speak your mind clearly.

Celestite is better suited for enhancing your inner spirituality. Turquoise helps eliminate much of your negative energy and the electromagnetic smog that exudes from the environment. This will allow for clearer thinking, leaving you with calmer nerves, especially when having to speak publicly.

Indigo

Indigo is often associated with your "third eye." It enhances your perception and intuition. That coupled with an improved understanding and a deep sense of calm can be achieved by working with indigo. The azurite crystal frees up those long-term blocks in communication and will aid in revealing whatever it is that is getting in the way of us reaching our full potential. In addition, you can look forward to a better memory too.

Violet

These tap into your creative side, improving your imagination, and whatever it is that inspires you. You get the empathy you need to feel more connected with others and it can help to rebalance your body, pulling you away from emotional extremes. Amethyst, one of the most practical of the violet crystals, can be used in a wide range of applications. Used with meditation, it gives you a sense of quietness and helps to clear the mind. It paves the way for lucid dreaming and serves as a block against computer and electromagnetic stresses you may not be aware of. This gives you an improved mental clarity, so you can be much more efficient at what you need to do.

White

Clear stones (or white stones) allow you to reflect all the other energies that surround you. It is directly related to your abilities in clarity, cleansing, and purification. A clear quartz, for example, can give your energy levels a boost, channel exterior energies to you, help to absorb, store, amplify, balance, and even focus on other energies. This aids your ability to heal, meditate, and manifest your individual qualities.

The moonstone has a soft luminescence about it that is perfect for helping to ease tensions that result from emotional disturbances. It can help to improve digestive issues or anywhere else where your body's fluids may be out of balance.

Black

The black stones work the opposite of the white. Black stones will reveal to you the hidden potentials of the circumstances that surround you. They help to manifest and give you a solid perspective of a situation. Because they can absorb light, they hold all of the energies inside. It requires patience to use a black stone. They help you to ground yourself and serve as an anchor so that you can function normally. In time, you will uncover many different hidden aspects of your life so that you can deal with them more effectively. In that respect, black stones have more of a purifying role than anything else.

The smoky quartz is a protective stone that is able to help dissolve any negative states that surround you. Using it will help you to attain a deeper level of who you really are inside and then allow you to cleanse and balance your beings. It is for this reason that many black stones can be very practical to use when practicing meditation.

There are many more ways you can benefit from the use of crystals. As you can see from the above examples, they all have different ways to help you heal. It is not like a medication prescribed by a doctor that only has one purpose. Crystals can be used in a wide range of areas and you're not limited to a single one. As you grow in your knowledge of these gems, you'll come to a much better understanding of how you can use them to your advantage.

Eliminates Negative Energy

All of us have good days and bad days from time to time. But when you find that you're in a constant spiral of negativity, it can be a difficult struggle to break free. No human action taken in this world happens if it hasn't been thought about first. Every action appears first as a thought, then an emotion, before it actually happens, so to eliminate the negative energy that you're struggling with, you first must harness those negative thoughts.

We all understand the power of negative people. If you don't do something to stop the spiraling effect, then chances are, you'll end up in a cyclone of bad feelings, which will eventually disrupt your mental and physical abilities, taking it down the tubes with you. But all of this is not so easily done.

First, you must surround yourself with positive energy, but that's not always possible. For this kind of help, it is best to use crystals. After you've done everything you can physically to resolve or change your situation, you can turn to crystals to help to neutralize this negativity. There are several different crystals that can do this quite effectively.

Probably the most powerful of these is the Black Tourmaline crystal. It is the go-to piece that many people rely on. Simply by placing in nearby while you're in a negative situation can help to cut down on a great deal of the dark energy flooding your environment. It is very effective at blocking electromagnetic fields that are in the air from all of the electronic devices we have come to depend on.

Black Tourmaline, however, can be quite a formidable piece of stone. While a larger stone may be your favored piece, carrying it around with you can be cumbersome. Instead, many people choose to have amulets, bracelets, and pendants made from it so that it is more practical and less obvious to others. It works by putting an invisible protective shield around you that can block a lot of that negative energy from getting in your way.

Another similar stone used to eliminate negative energy is the black obsidian. This stone is extremely powerful and may not be a good option for regular use. Many crystal users actually prefer the gentleness of the black tourmaline over the black obsidian for that purpose.

Smoky quartz can also be effective in protecting you from negative energy. In addition to keeping the negative energy from overwhelming you, it is also a great way to detox you from the inside out. Any negative thoughts that are hovering just below the surface can easily begin to fester and foster new negativity in your life without you realizing it. The longer it goes undetected, the deeper and denser it gets, until it begins to manifest itself in some physical way (headaches, stomach aches, colds, flu, etc.)

A good defense mechanism is to have a combination of both stones working together. You can have them made into a nice bracelet or pendant that you can wear at all times. Some even take them along in a little pouch that they can keep in their backpack or purse.

To further enhance your forcing out of negativity, you can use your crystals along with essential oils. Sage, orange, and tangerine scents are very effective at lifting a positive mood. It can be very difficult to stay in a negative frame of mind when you are surrounded by the scent of citrus in the air. It can quickly change the mood of any number of bad situations.

Other very effective options for pushing out negativity are bergamot and ylang-ylang. So whether you choose to use black tourmaline, black obsidian, or smoky quartz, the next time you need to neutralize the negativity infiltrating your space, choose one, a combination, or a mix of the stone with essential oils, and you should see an almost immediate effect.

Reenergize Mind and Body

As we've already explained, crystals, like everything else, are infused with a constantly vibrating energy. This energy flows through every cell in our bodies. But in addition to this energy, our cells also contain very specific energy patterns. When we are under stress, we tend to take up unhealthy habits that can lead to illnesses and other physical problems. When this happens, the energy that flows within you can be interrupted or at the very least compromised.

In using crystals to help reenergize the mind and body, we need to understand our body composition better. Since we are all composed of around 70% water, we can use this knowledge to help us to heal correctly.

This type of healing can be done in many ways. Since each crystal is composed of natural minerals found in the earth, and our bodies are mostly comprised of the most precious liquid found on the earth, by simply holding a crystal in our hands, we can allow its energy to connect with the water in our bodies and make it possible to infuse ourselves with more energy.

Many people like to say a chant, a mantra, or some type of phrase to activate the power of the mind to work with the crystals. While there are many books that will provide you with a chant or phrase to use in these instances, the best results come from words that have been specifically tailored to your personal circumstances. For example, you might want to say something like:

"I feel energized in my heart, mind, and soul. Every day, my body will achieve its optimum health no matter what the circumstances."

You can hold a crystal stone in your hand or you can simply touch a necklace made with the stone. As you say it, your energies will be transferred to the necklace or stone. Once done, take the necklace and drape it around a glass of water and wait until the water is energized from the stone. Some like to take the water and place it outside in the direct sunlight and wait for at least 4 hours before drinking it. In this way, you begin to slowly reprogram your mind and body.

Other ways to reenergize your mind and body with crystals is to try a few techniques with different stones.

Turquoise: The beautiful blue of the turquoise usually has a little black flowing through it. These stones are most effective in diffusing depression, fears, anxiety, and even physical exhaustion. If you're practicing meditation, turquoise can help to bring you balance and restore positive thoughts to your mind.

Amethyst: If you've lost your energy because of stress, an amethyst can be very powerful in restoring energy balance back in your life. Especially if you're going through the loss of a loved one, a divorce, or insomnia.

The lavender amethyst helps to keep the hormones in balance, stimulate the immune system, and gives your metabolism a boost all at the same time. It's is great for relieving stress and even some physical problems you might suffer as a result of that stress (headaches).

Blue Topaz: Helps to keep the fifth Chakra in balance. When this is in balance, you will have better communication skills, feel happier, and will naturally be drawn to things that will bring you success. It is a powerful stone that is strong enough to strengthen your nerves, improve your digestion, and reenergize the whole body at the same time.

Other stones that are effective in reenergizing the body are rubies, amazonite, citrine, rose quartz, crystal quartz, onyx, and moonstone.

Feel More Relaxed and Centered

There are also many calming crystals you can use to help you relieve chronic stress. When your stress and anxiety levels get out of control, rather than turning to traditional medicine, think of using crystals as your first go-to treatment. They work just as well as deep breathing exercises can when infusing oxygen to the brain.

Start by taking the time to meditate on a regular basis. This helps to open the door to an inner peace and give you a mental refuge from the world. Since there are so many crystals that can help to calm and center you, we suggest that you start by experimenting with several of them until you find the one that 'talks to you' in a way that you understand. Once you find the one that fits you personally, start incorporating it into your meditation practice.

As a beginner, here are a few you can start off with.

- Blue Lace Agate
- Lepidolite
- Amethyst
- Angelite
- Flourite
- Black Tourmaline

The Blue Lace Agate, for example, has a beautiful periwinkle color that has a very calming vibration that can bring you peace of mind. Holding it daily can calm your nerves and lower your anxiety. If you tend to have frequent anxiety, try wearing it as a bracelet or carrying one around in your pocket.

Lepidolite is partially composed of naturally occurring lithium, which is often used as an anti-anxiety medication. Jet stones fight against negative emotions like grief and stress and work like a suit of armor, protecting you from many of the external things that can negatively impact your mind, body, and spirit.

As you continue on in your study of crystals, you will find there are many that have a calming effect that can help to ease your anxiety. Experiment with several of them and choose those that speak to you. You may be a beginner when it comes to using crystals, but you were born with an internal intuition that will help you decide if you allow it to guide you. If you find that you can touch, feel, and get an effect from any one of the crystals you try, you should be well on your way down the path to true crystal healing.

CHAPTER 4
Crystals And Chakras

It's true that you can do a lot with crystals without any knowledge of your chakras and how they work. However, if you're really serious about learning how to use crystals to your advantage, you should know at least a little about chakras. It can only help to enhance your healing and bring you more powerful effects.

The 7 Chakras in the Body

Chakras make up the key energy centers of the body. We already talked about each of these centers:

- The first chakra sits at the base of the tailbone
- The second chakra sits near the navel
- The third chakra sits at the base of the sternum
- The fourth chakra sits right in the middle of the chest
- The fifth chakra sits in the throat directly above the Adam's apple
- The sixth chakra sits in the center of the forehead, between the eyes
- The seventh chakra sits at the very top of the crown of the head

These are the body's main chakras, but they are not all of them. Your chakras are located throughout the body, however, these are the primary ones and a good place for a beginner to get started.

Energy flows in and out of your body through chakras, but at times, the flow of energy can become blocked through one or more of these chakras, giving you an unbalanced flow of energy. These blockages can be a direct result of trauma, illness, or lifestyle practices you may have. You may not be aware that your chakra is blocked, but there will be evidence of it if you know what to look for.

For example, you may begin to have emotional problems, an unexplained physical pain, or a health issue that doesn't seem to want to go away, no matter what you do. When the root chakra is blocked, you may start to experience lower back pain. If the heart chakra is blocked, you may develop heart problems or find yourself stuck in an emotional downfall.

Each of the chakras has its own corresponding color, which directly correlates to the frequency of vibration of its energy. So if you are working with both crystals and chakras together, make sure you choose the colors that best match the chakra you are trying to heal.

Why They Work

With both major and minor chakras, if it is not working properly or if it has become blocked, our overall health and well-being will begin to suffer. Generally, if you are feeling physically, emotionally, or psychologically off balance, you can be pretty sure that something is wrong with one of your chakras. If you are feeling down, it could be the result of not getting enough energy to support your needs. If you are blocking negative feelings, you may be unconsciously interfering with a healthy flow of energy.

On the other hand, if you are working hard on balancing your emotional, mental, physical, and spiritual health, you can better accomplish your goals by balancing the flow of energy through your chakras. The trick is to know how to tap into that chakra when needed.

One way to make this work is by regularly practicing yoga. If you've ever practiced yoga, then you know how one simple movement can clear your head of all sorts of clutter, physically and emotionally. This is because that move opened up the pathways to that chakra. The more you understand the unique properties of chakras, the easier it will be to see exactly how they work.

The Root Chakra or the Muladhara: This chakra is related to your survival and the ability to feel safe and secure. Located right at the base of the spine, its associated color is red. Because it is the lowest of the major chakras, it sits closest to the earth. In order to maintain a healthy Muladhara, you need to perform exercises that are closely related to the earth like dancing, jogging, and jumping. The combination of those movements with the crystals will help to put your mind at ease. Once you begin to see the world as a safe place, the chakra will open up to a flood of energetic vibrations.

The Sacral Chakra or the Svadhistana: The second chakra is closely related to your sensuality, sexuality, and your internal desire for pleasure. It is located right in the lower abdomen and its associated color is orange. Exercises that work well with your Svadhistana are belly dancing and yoga. It also helps to be involved in a loving partnership to enhance its effects on your energy flow. When the energy flows freely through this chakra, you are better able to live your dreams and do whatever is necessary to make them your reality.

Solar Plexus Chakra or Manipura: The Manipura's associated color is yellow and it is directly connected to your view of your power in the world. When you have an overbearing personality, out of sync with the other chakras in your body, you can develop some very negative tendencies like obsessive-compulsive disorders (OCD) for example. However, if your energy flow through this region is healthy, you will feel more empowered and you'll have better control over these types of disorders.

Heart Chakra or Anahata: With the associated color of green, this chakra is directly connected to your feelings of love and compassion. It's also associated with the natural element of air. When you have healthy relationships with family, friends, even animals, your heart energy flows freely. Even when you have that spiritual connection with nature and its beauty, the energy from this chakra can be very strong. It allows you to not only give love when you feel it but to accept it as well.

Throat Chakra or Vishuddha: This chakra has an energy that flows through your words. It is the energy of communication. Its associated color is blue. When the energy flows freely through this region, you can speak with confidence, asking for what you need without reservation. It also reflects your truth. Exercises that build up this chakra are singing, chanting, and breathing.

The Third Eye Chakra or the Ajna: The Third Eye's natural color is indigo. It is the gateway of the energy that controls your insight, intuition, and awareness. Situated right between the eyebrows, exercises that work best with Ajna are meditation and visualization, which can aid in the healthy flow of energy in this region.

The Crown Chakra or the Sahasrara: This chakra energizes your spiritual connection. Its associated color is violet. It supports unity, blissfulness, and the knowledge that you own. This chakra allows you to be consciously aware of elements in your life and allow you to be at peace with them.

If you're planning to use crystals along with your chakras, to get the best effect and better energy flow from each one, use the exercises suggested with each one. As you can see, understanding the chakras can help in breathing new energy into your body. It is best to start with your base chakra, seeing and using the associated colors to get your energies flowing in an uninterrupted and healthy way.

Some people prefer to start off with meditation to get their minds focused on the purpose with each session. It is one of the best means of helping your body's energy to flow the way it was originally designed to do.

Chakra Connections

Each chakra has a unique mode of expression and will show you a different picture of life. At times, your work with chakras will involve more than yourself. When making a chakra connection with another person (as in a relationship), you communicate by sending your energy from you to the other person and vice versa.

If you are sending energy from the right side of your body, they should be receiving it on their left side. In such cases, the flow in both of your bodies remains balanced. However, this kind of energy transmission is not always necessary, nor is it always possible. If either one of you has a blockage in one or more of your chakras, the communication you are sending can be blocked as well. There are several steps you can take to correct this situation.

When you use crystals to heal a chakra, everything will begin to work correctly. These chakras are found in a straight line that runs right up the center of the body. To make the best use of your crystals, place it right where the chakra is located. There are specific healing crystals that work well with connecting to the natural properties of the chakra. They can amplify the energy that is flowing through the region, open it, or even heal it. So try to find the crystal that works best with the chakra you're trying to help.

The Root: Its primary color is red but grey and black are also closely associated with it. Look for stones of these colors like bloodstone, garnet, onyx, ruby, and red jasper.

The Navel: It has an orange color so crystals that work best with it are carnelian, goldstone, orange zincite, or tangerine quartz.

The Solar Plexus: Look for stones that match its yellow color like citrine, sapphire, picture jasper, yellow calcite, and yellow sapphire.

The Heart: It can be green or pink so crystals like green calcite, pink morganite, rose quartz, and green tourmaline works best.

The Throat: Use blue crystals like turquoise or aqua. You can use any shade of blue, but try to choose the lighter shades like blue lace agate, aquamarine, and angelite.

The Brow: The colors to look for here are indigo and any of the darker blue shades like lapis lazuli, sodalite, and the hawk's eye.

The Crown: A violet or purple color crystal that can radiate out its clear or white color. Look for stones like amethyst and clear quartz.

Balancing Chakras

It is important to choose a crystal that will vibrate at the same frequency as the chakra. This will help to clear the blockage and restore the flow of energy through the body. It works well to heal a wide range of spiritual, emotional, mental, and physical challenges that may have developed as a result of the blockage.

To use the crystals properly, take the following steps:

- Lie on your back with eyes closed.
- Place the crystal on the blocked chakra.
- With eyes closed, visualize the color of the chakra and imagine the energy as it flows free of interruptions.
- Each chakra will yield different results to help you to know when you have freed the blockage.

First Chakra: Allows you to connect to your emotions, feel more secure and safe, and have a sense of belonging in your community.

Second Chakra: Will give you a stronger sense of personal power, sexuality, and tap into your creative side.

Third Chakra: Improved self-esteem, a sense of prosperity, better self-identity, and a stronger sense of morals.

Fourth Chakra: You will have more emotional balance, you'll love easier, be more forgiving, and more compassionate.

Fifth Chakra: Better self-expression, communicate with others more easily, be more honest, and have a stronger sense of integrity.

Sixth Chakra: A heightened sense of intuition, better insight, stronger beliefs and attitudes, and you'll have a clearer mind than before.

Seventh Chakra: A stronger connection to the spiritual world, a heightened consciousness, and a feeling that you are connected to the universe, a sense of oneness with other things outside of yourself.

This type of crystal energy, when used in the right way can have a major impact on every aspect of your life. If you allow it, it can take you on a spiritual journey that will help you to move beyond the physical and become a part of the bigger picture of life. In order for all of this to happen, you have to approach your work with crystals with the right intentions.

This is not a practice that can no longer be relegated to the mystic world. Science has zeroed in on the power of crystals and has used it to their advantage. How it works can best be explained by IBM scientist, Marcel Vogel. He observed crystals growing under a microscope and made an intriguing observation. As he watched, he noticed that they took on the shape of whatever he was thinking about. This was the first significant realization that crystals were transmitting energy to the human mind and was receiving energy from humans.

Even Albert Einstein recognized the vibrations of everything that exists in our world. Just like you can't see sound waves, your thoughts emit vibrations that impact other things in your life. Therefore, with crystals to enhance our feelings, emotions, and thoughts, amplifying them in the right way, we can have the ability to change our lives and transform them into something that can keep us in balance, so we can literally embrace life and the abundance of opportunities they have for us.

CHAPTER 5
Crystal Grids

Now that you understand the fundamentals of crystals and chakras and how they work, we can go on to applying this information with crystal grids. To put it simply, a crystal grid is a method of working with crystals that involves creating very specific arrangements of different geometric shapes or patterns. These patterns usually include some type of sacred geometry in their form.

When used properly, these grids can amplify the power of the crystals even more. While it is possible to get good results from the use of a single crystal, when you use a grid, it can only enhance the results and give its energy a significant boost.

To create your own crystal grid, you first need to establish a foundation or a base to work with. The shape you use can be printed on a piece of fabric or a paper. Some have engraved wooden boards that they can lay out to place their crystals on. In some cases, you can even obtain a template to show you exactly where to place your crystals for the best effect.

Why You Need Them

You can use a crystal grid for many different reasons. Some people use them primarily for spiritual connections, but they can also be used for healing, to provide protection, to find love, to achieve prosperity, or any other number of things.

When you use the crystal grid, the collection of crystals all working together has an increased power that works alongside the sacred geometry to harness extra energy to work on your behalf. They also serve as a solid anchor when you need them.

As you can probably imagine, there are many ways to create a crystal grid, each with its own unique benefits to you. While there may be many reasons to justify using a grid, we can break them down into four different categories.

Crystal Energy: Because of their unique structure, crystals work really well when used in certain patterns. The crystal grid helps to harness even more of their properties to give you added support in accomplishing your goal.

It is important to choose those crystals that have the very properties you're searching for. To achieve your intended purpose, you may have to think beyond the obvious though. If for example, you are looking to improve your chances of success, then you would obviously choose crystals that will help you to achieve that goal, but you could also include crystals with related properties like determination, prosperity, and self-confidence to support it. Together, the power of all of these elements can help to direct their energy in the right direction for you.

Sacred Geometry: There is a form of metaphysical science that supports the belief that certain patterns that are found in nature are actually a fingerprint for understanding the universe and how everything in it actually works. These shapes are referred to as sacred geometry and they represent the actual framework of all creation.

Each of these shapes has their own use and form of energy. While not every crystal grid uses sacred geometry, when it does, it makes the entire grid far more powerful than one that does not. When using sacred geometry, choose your grids very carefully to ensure that the power you will receive will be directed towards your actual purpose.

Using sacred geometry also is beneficial in helping you to transmit your energies out of the grid into the rest of the universe so that the results can be manifested. You can also channel that energy inward to heal your broken aura to improve yourself when needed. The point is that while crystals have their own unique powers that can help you, using them with specific chakras within a grid can enhance their power even more. If you use a crystal grid with sacred geometry, you get the most intense power possible in the metaphysical world.

Numerology: Crystal grids used with the ancient spiritual science of numerology is very similar to sacred geometry. By selecting the number of crystals based on their symbolic meaning and energy as it relates to the grid, you can connect to support your purpose and better connect to their energy. Not only does this amplify the energy emanating from them, but it channels it better to focus on a very specific task.

Your Intention: Don't forget the power and the energy that is generated by your own thoughts. When you can transmit that information to crystals, especially when they have been carefully placed on a grid, this is when they really work their best. You can program your crystals with your thoughts and dreams. The grid will store them and broadcast them out into the universe for as long as you need them to.

These grids can become powerful tools in your hands and are extremely effective. However, in order for you to get the best results, you must follow through on any intentions you transmit to them. Their power is a source of energy and motivation, but you will not receive rewards for anything that you don't wish to work on. They can only connect to something that is real within you and broadcast that intention around the clock for as long as you need them to in order to effect the change that you need.

Helps to Harness Power

It is not enough that you are able to amplify the power of the crystals in a grid. While all that additional energy can be a huge benefit to you, you need to harness it and direct its energies in a way that it will truly heal your chakras in a more focused manner.

When you start your grid by selecting only those crystals that will enhance and push your intentions out into the universe, in such a way that their energies become complements of each other, the solution to your problem often becomes very clear. As a result of harnessing this plethora of power, you will no longer need to worry about a conflict of energies or if the crystals have been arranged in a manner that might even restrict their powers. Rather, this harnessed energy can be channeled in any direction you wish it.

In essence, using crystal grids in the right way can literally put the power of the universe into your hands.

How to Create a Crystal Grid

To get started, it is important that you carefully select the crystals you plan to use on the grid. There are many different ways to choose the stones, but most experts believe that the stone actually chooses you rather than the other way around. Remember, you are tapping into the powers of the universe and connecting them to the energies inside of you. This is not a decision that is made purely in your head, you will have to involve your own intuition along with your logic in making this decision.

When you go shopping for your new crystals, walk around the room and casually observe each crystal there. Study its shape, color, and patterns carefully and wait for one of them to pull you in. Because each crystal has its own unique vibration, when one connects with you, you will notice it if you are paying attention.

Choosing the right stone requires patience and a quiet mind. When a particular stone pulls you in, maybe by the intricacy of its pattern, its color, or its shape, pick it up. Hold it in your hand and think about your purpose. If it is the right stone for you, you should begin to feel sensations in your hand. Some report that they feel a warmth come over them, others say it is cold. Other possible sensations you might feel are soft pulsations, a sense of calm and tranquility. All of these are signs that the stone you're holding is the one that is calling to you.

Therefore, choosing the stone requires knowing your intent before you begin. It doesn't really matter what your intention is, you will be much more successful in using crystals if you have it clearly in mind. Your thoughts have their own vibrations that emanate throughout the universe. This means that one of the most valuable tools you'll have at your disposal is your own mind. This will provide you with insight and help you to live better in the present.

Your intentions or purpose works like a magnet, attracting what will make them come true. Preparing your mind to choose a crystal is an extremely important step that helps crystals to align themselves to your values and purpose of life.

- First, decide what is most important to you.
- Explore different areas of your life that you feel need improvement.
- Be very specific in clarifying your needs and when you want to see them come true.
- Write them down in the present tense.

Once you have your intention clearly written down in front of you, they begin to take on a physical life of their own. They are now starting to become real and as a result, will help guide you to the right crystals.

Cleanse and charge your crystals: Because of their highly energetic properties, crystals will react to any energy pattern they come in contact with. By the time you get your crystal home, it has probably been touched by hundreds of different hands. So one of the first things you need to do is cleanse the crystal and then do a weekly cleaning afterward.

There are several different ways you can cleanse your crystals. Here are a few suggestions:

- Soak them in salt water. Let them remain submerged in the salt water solution for a minimum of one hour. Make sure you use Himalayan pink salt rather than regular table salt for the best effect. Do not use this method of cleaning for porous stones like rose and gypsum as the saltwater could cause damage. You also want to avoid using salt water on magnetic stones like lodestone. The salt could cause portions of the stone to rust.

- You can also smoke them by burning a small bundle of sage, cedar, lavender, or sweetgrass. Set fire to these dried plants and then once they begin to produce smoke, extinguish the flame. Hold the crystals in the tendril of smoke to cleanse them. You can use only one of these herbs or all four if you like. If you don't have those herbs, then consider using incense instead.

- If you practice some type of special healing skills like Reiki, you can use your own energy to cleanse them.

Be careful. Crystals are amazing pieces of nature, they will never lose their energy. Even if by chance, you should break one, the source of its energy is still there. The only real way to bring about the demise of a crystal is to not clean it. As it comes in contact with more and more people, it will begin to take on the energy of everyone who touched it, for the good or for the bad. Without cleaning it on a regular basis, you're leaving yourself vulnerable to possible negative energies flowing in and out of you.

Once your crystals have been properly cleaned, they need to be charged or programmed. This restores it back to its natural condition, so they can continue along using their energy on your behalf. Every time you cleanse your crystals, they also need to be charged.

This involves putting your own personal intentions into them. In other words, you need to give your crystals a job to do. It is up to you to transmit your thoughts, intentions, and purposes to the crystals. This is important as you will inevitably have times when you will be vibrating at a very low frequency. Those are the times when you will be feeling down, depressed, and unfulfilled in some way. When that happens, your intentions can easily evaporate. However, if your intentions have been transmitted to the crystal, when you reconnect with it, your purpose can be restored and you can more quickly get back on the right track.

Programming your crystal is relatively simple. After cleaning, take the crystal and hold it in both hands, close your eyes, and take three deep, slow breaths in and out. Meditate on your faith, the Earth, and all those things that make you happy, give you contentment and satisfaction in life. These thoughts will take your body to a higher vibration, which is the frequency that is more connected to a spiritual or religious belief. The belief in something that has a power that is far greater than anything you can produce on your own. For some people, this spiritual vibration is more of a scientific connection. Whatever it is for you, it is up to you to tap into this vibration. When you do, ask the crystal to clear itself of all unwanted energies or previous programming it may have once held, so it will be clear of everything but what you put into it.

However you choose to say it, verbalize your intent. Speaking out loud, you might say something like the following words. *"I am requesting that the highest vibrations found in love and light join with my highest vibrations and work together to clear away any unwanted energy or any previous programming it may have received. I order this crystal to hold my intentions of ...."*

You can complete the phrase by adding three very specific intentions of your own for the crystal to follow through with. You can give it any intentions you want. You finish the programming by saying "thank you" three times. By offering thanks three times, it is your way of emphasizing that what you want to achieve is in fact, possible in the universe.

The Elements of a Crystal Grid

Once your crystals have been cleansed and programmed, you are ready to start forming your grid. While each grid is unique to you and your purpose, there are some very basic elements that you must have for it to work properly. When all of these elements are combined, the grid can produce a powerful but synergistic blend of energies. Knowing which crystals can be used and where they can be placed on the pattern requires some level of understanding about crystal energy as well as the universal patterns of life. As you create your grid, you must make sure that it has these components:

The Path: the direction of how the energy will flow inside the grid

The Design: An energy path that will work with the objective or purpose of the grid

The Visuals: These would include a balance of the designs and colors, any words or images that will enhance the aesthetic of the grid and give you the desired feeling when you are in contact with it.

The Elements: The actual crystals you will be using on the grid. These include the Focus Stone, Way Stones, Spirit Stones, Desire Stones, and Perimeter Stones. We'll discuss each of these a little later in this chapter.

The Wand: The tool you use in order to activate the grid.

The Path: The path is based on a pretty basic principle. It is the direction you want the energy to follow throughout the grid. A well-designed path will have a clearly laid out direction for the energy to follow so that it can be concentrated and directed towards one single point on the grid.

The Design: The design or the layout for the grid can take on a number of possible shapes and forms. While you are free to create a design at random, the most effective grids rely on sacred geometry and use only those forms you can actually find in nature. We could dedicate an entire book to each of these shapes and what they mean, but you can easily access information about many of these online and find a sacred geometrical shape that will match your purpose. These can be downloaded and printed out and used as a base pattern for your grid whenever you need them.

However, as a beginner, you can start with some of the most commonly used designs to create your grid.

- **The Circle:** Represents completeness, divine will, unity, purposeful action, singularity, inclusion and/or new beginnings.
- **The Vesica Piscis** (*which looks like two circles intertwined*): Represents bringing together opposites. It

can be used to bridge misunderstandings, join the spirit and the body together, or to unite a number of things that have been divided. It is also used to heal emotional wounds.

- **Tripod of Life** (*which looks like three circles intertwined, two on the top and one underneath*): Represents balance in life. It centers, unites, and stabilizes groups of three elements. The mind, body, and spirit for example, or the past, present, and future.

- **Seed of Life** (*appears with multiple circles intertwined and held within one larger circle*)**:** Represents the completion of a task or the achievement of a specific goal. It can also reflect harmony, balance, sincerity, and truth. In essence, it is a sacred geometrical shape that can be used for a wide number of things.

The Visuals: Once you have chosen your design, the next step is to enhance the aesthetics of your grid by adding visuals to it. While the design we spoke about above is one area of aesthetics, you can also add other visuals to emphasize your purpose or intent.

For example, you might want to consider using the colors of the crystals to help form more aesthetically pleasing patterns or add color to your grid in some other way that connects to your intention. Many people add color in the form of flowers, pictures, colored text, candles, etc. This added color is not limited to the crystal stones and can come from anywhere.

You can also create a vision board and place your grid on top of it. A common practice is to use images that relate closely to your purpose or vision. These could include health and wellness, wealth and prosperity, career fulfillment, close and loving relationships, etc.

Affirmations: Affirmations are powerful tools you can use at any time, but combining them with a crystal grid can make them even more powerful. By writing down an affirmation that specifically relates to the purpose of the grid, you draw the attention of the powers that exist in the physical realm to your purpose and can receive the support through the energies in the grid.

The Elements: When it comes time to actually start putting the grid together, you need to make sure that you have very specific elements in place. Each crystal will have its own purpose. You will need to have a focus stone, way stones, spirit stones, and desire stones. All of these will fit inside a series of stones called the perimeter.

Make sure that the crystals you select are chosen based on their ability to amplify and focus the energy in the direction of your purpose or intention. Which crystals you choose will depend on the elements of each crystal itself. Your decision could be based on the color, its power of influence, or its shape.

- **The Focus Stone:** Every grid needs to have a center crystal referred to as the Focus Stone, which works like an anchor for the entire grid, then you must choose several other stones to work with that one. The purpose of the focus stone is to gather energy from the other surrounding stones, from the universe, and then channel it back into the grid. This creates a downward flow of coherent energy. Any energy that emanates from the Focus Stone will be modified and reshaped by the power produced from the crystal grid.

- **The Way Stones:** The Way Stones are placed around the Focus Stone and laid out on a specific path. They work to modify the energies that emanate from the Focus Stone and then amplify and modify any energy that is coming into the grid from outside.

- **The Desire Stones:** These are placed on the outermost section of the grid and signify your desires, goals, or purposes that you want to achieve. They can also gather energy, especially from areas that have been channeled and modified by the Focus and Way stones. You could consider these stones as a means of fine-tuning the energies channeled from the other crystals. Select your desire stones in the same way as you would your Way Stones. Look at their color rays and the energy lattice. These are usually the same stones you would select to use outside of the grid. You know, the ones you carry with you throughout the day to help you achieve a specific goal. However, you can considerably amplify their power by using them in a crystal grid.

- **The Path:** This is the path of energy that flows through the grid. Its purpose is to channel the energy from the Focus Stone to the Way Stones and then on to the Desire Stones. It's a representation of the journey you must take in order to achieve the object or action of your desire. The path will be directed by the shape of the grid, so you can enhance its specific powers and meanings. There are many directions the path must take. Some will go in a very familiar direction like in a circle, square, or a triangle. Others will take on more complex directions like hexagons, pentagons or even spirals. Do a little added research to determine which path will work best for your purpose. Rarely will you find one that leads you in a straight line. There are many others besides the one mentioned here, that are very useful and can add even more power to your crystal grid.

When creating a crystal grid, it is best to first visualize yourself engaging in your desired activity. If you are building a grid that will help you to become more profitable, you might visualize yourself with the money or the material things you are trying to attain. If your goal is to find love in your life, visualize yourself in a happy family environment.

Let's Lay It All Out

Just as important as all of the elements of your crystal grid, is the location you place the grid. You will need to find a location where it won't be disturbed while it does its work. Keep it in a place away from kids, animals, and anything else that could somehow accidentally alter its shape once it's been set up.

Start with a small piece of paper and write down your intention. Make sure that your words are very specific because this will help you to make a better choice on which crystals are needed in the grid. While there are no right answers for which stones to choose, always go for the ones that are calling or speaking to you.

Next, cleanse the space where the grid will be by burning palo santo or sage. The smoke will purify the area before you begin laying everything out.

Take the paper that you wrote your intentions on, fold it and place it in the center of the grid.

Take several deep breaths while you have your intentions clearly in mind. State those intentions out loud. Then start to create your grid.

Begin by forming the outside first and move towards the center. It is important for you to keep focusing on your purpose while you place each stone in place.

Finally, place your Focus Stone on top of the paper with your intentions written on it.

Congratulations! Your crystal grid is finally finished. Now it's time to activate it!

The Wand: To activate the grid, use a quartz crystal point, which is a special crystal with a pencil-like point on the end that radiates pure white light into your grid. These are some of the most powerful crystals you can find for focusing on and amplifying your purpose.

With your point, connect each crystal in the grid by drawing an invisible and unbroken line to each of them. Start with the outside crystals and don't stop until you connect every one of them to the center Focus Stone. After they are all connected, your grid is fully activated. It is important that you keep your grid until your intention has been fulfilled.

Once you have achieved your purpose, you might want to keep it up a little longer to show your thanks and appreciation for the help, but eventually, you'll want to make other grids and your focus will end up being directed to other places. You are now ready to move on to other things in the world of crystals.

CHAPTER 6
Why You Should Learn/Practice Crystal Healing

If you're not entirely convinced of the power of crystals, you tend to be more cynical about their worth. There are a few points you should be aware of. Most people who fall into this category tend to be those that are still of the mind that crystal healing should be relegated to the old school of thought associating it with magic, mysticism, and even a fragment left over from the hippie era of the 1960s. While that was the way it once was viewed, because of new science, we can now give it a more prominent and proven role in our lives.

Rather than thinking of it as a connection to the spirit world, think of it merely as a means of bringing our lives in tune with the more abstract aspects of our universe. Since we already know that everything in the universe is in a constantly vibrating state, including us humans, it is only logical to see that things will work better with fewer problems if those vibrations are in harmony with each other.

Your relationship with your crystals is a highly personal one and if you use them as tools to bring you that harmony, you will find a new approach to solving any personal, financial, physical, emotional, or psychological issues you face.

When we say that everything in the universe is vibrating at a different frequency, we mean everything. You may be one person, but you are made up of different parts. Your organs, chakras, and your thoughts are all vibrating differently as well. In essence, your body is a symphony of vibrations that you are trying to get to work together to create the rhythm of your life. Crystals have a unique way of making this happen. By embracing their unique and clear vibrations, they can work to harmonize your life in much the same way as a piano tuner tunes the different keys on the piano. They can recalibrate all of your vibrations, so they blend much better together. This will help you to be more balanced emotionally, physically, mentally, and spiritually.

While you may be drawn to crystals for their unique color or intricate patterns, in time, you will learn that much more was involved in your choice. As you connect and learn more about your crystal, you will learn about its specific purpose and energy and you'll discover that it wasn't you that chose it, but that it chose you. These stones bring about a certain type of balance that is difficult to achieve in any other way in the world.

Later, we'll discuss some of the most prominent stones and how they can benefit you personally. As you learn more about the properties of different crystals, you'll find that you will be a better gauge of what will work right for you and why.

It's Effects on the Body

Even now, in the face of modern science, medical professionals are beginning to see that crystal healing is a perfect complementary form of treatment. When used in this way, they help many to understand why they are so important. Here are some facts that we must keep in mind.

1. Our human body is merely a collection of different energy fields with their own energy centers or chakras. While it may feel solid to us, parts of our body are made up of light and liquid. Each of these parts is vibrating at a different frequency.

2. Crystals have their own vibrations, which can have a direct effect on the flow of energy that surrounds our body. Surrounding our body are electromagnetic fields that we refer to as our aura. In addition to this aura are the seven major chakras, which have a direct effect on the different areas in our physical body. Our external aura is an outward reflection of the health of our physical body and the flow of energy through our chakras. If our aura is bright, it means that the energy flowing through our chakras is strong and uninterrupted. On the other hand, if our aura is dim, it means that we have some sort of blockage that needs to be cleared.

This is why many people have been able to successfully treat even severe cases of depression with crystal therapy. Through this type of therapy, it was observed that the aura was dimmed or otherwise damaged. On further examination, these were patients that had a) undergone some type of trauma that caused an energy imbalance, b) underwent chemotherapy, or c) had been given a drug of some type to deal with extreme pain. In all of these cases, recovery from the physical damage done could take an extremely long time with traditional western treatment and medication. In the meantime, the patient often struggles with a loss of vitality and maybe even an inability to cope with everyday life. However, with crystal therapy, these imbalances have the potential of improving much faster and in a more natural way.

It is the subtle vibrations that each of these crystals has that makes this type of healing possible. They have a way of re-energizing the body's energy fields. When you use the right crystal for your specific needs, amazing things can happen. The more you learn about these beautiful gems, the sooner the healing process can begin. When you know intuitively how to find a blockage and which crystal to choose to free it, then you will feel more grounded and that's when you will receive the maximum benefits their healing energies can provide. As a result, you will be able to relax, easing up on all the stress in your life.

The Effects of Crystals on Emotions

It has often been reported that simply by placing crystals around you, can bring a great deal of comfort to an individual. When you are struggling with emotional issues, it is often because of being out of balance. By wearing crystals as jewelry or carrying them around with you every day, they can flood you with a continuous calming effect that you can't get from medication and all without those nasty side effects. They can be safely used in conjunction with a number of psychotherapeutic approaches without any negative consequences.

As crystals work on your imbalance, they can have a powerful impact on emotional healing. Whether you're suffering from extreme stress, anxiety, or some other negative emotions, you will find that there are certain crystals that will help you to cope better.

For example, many people use blue lace agate, jet, or black tourmaline to relieve anxiety and stress. Even for emotional trauma like coping with a breakup or a problem in their love life, they turn to rose quartz, lapis lazuli, or rhodonite.

When you are struggling with an extreme loss as in the case of the death of a loved one, you can also find comfort in amethyst, carnelian, or moonstones.

Anyone struggling with an extreme emotional issue should always consult with their doctor first. However, by working with crystals in tandem with your medical doctor, you can greatly enhance your recovery and heal yourself by balancing your energies. In many cases, this can be done through crystal therapy without the use of medications, which often work in ways that can be more harmful than good.

The Effects of Crystals on the Mind

Anyone who has struggled with negative thoughts knows that clearing the mind is not easy. However, crystal healing for mental clarity can be very effective in helping you to focus and push out all the negative mind chatter so you can get back to a more positive mental process. This is possible because of the multifarious powers that are held within each crystal. Whether you're trying to focus on something specific or you're trying to tap into your creative processes, there is a crystal that can help you through the process.

With accessing the energy in the crown chakra, you can activate your mental process and receive more mental clarity. While there are many crystals that can help you achieve this mental clarity, there are several that are much more powerful and can yield some pretty impressive results.

Amazonite: This stone is very effective for dealing with problems of absent-mindedness. Often this problem is the result of not being able to filter out things that are not important from your mind. Using amazonite in your presence can help you to have better communication and sensitivity in your thinking patterns. It also brings a calmer energy level that can prevent you from saying things without thinking and thus end up expressing thoughts you really didn't mean.

Malachite: This stone is very helpful for keeping your mental focus in check when life gets out of control. Often when things get hectic, you develop a negative cloud over you that can quickly force you to lose control. Malachite can help you to make the right decisions and focus more on the positive side of things rather than allowing your mind to drift off into a deep mental downward spiral. It can amplify your positive energy that can transform your mind into a more productive direction.

Clear Quartz: When you program clear quartz, it can hold any type of energy you need. It works best for those who find it difficult to concentrate on any one thing and helps them to take the kind of action that will allow their dreams to unfold. It forces you to repeat your resolutions again and again until you achieve your goals.

Hematite: If you're having trouble staying grounded mentally, Hematite can help you to get a more stable hold on your life. Regular meditation with this stone will help to put your mind back on the right track. You will be able to eliminate many of the wayward thoughts that overwhelm you, get rid of the negativity that is controlling you, and dispel the bad energy that may be surrounding you. As a result, you'll be more grounded and focused, so you can continue on your mental journey in a more positive direction.

Smoky Quartz: Smoky quartz is great for helping you to practice mindfulness. They work best when you take them out into the natural world helping you to focus on what's more important. As you let your mind absorb the energy of the smoky quartz, you'll be able to meditate better. You will be able to develop a positive train of thought and maintain it for a longer period of time. You'll also be able to avoid mental thoughts that are illogical and can lead to undue stress when you find yourself overwhelmed. In the end, you'll have a clearer mind that will allow you to focus on what's important and gloss over insignificant thoughts or those that bog you down in negativity.

It is recommended that you meditate on crystals for a minimum of three minutes or more every morning and then go about your day. These stones help you to be more consciously aware of everything you come in contact with throughout the day and allows you to find some positive contribution to give to them. Always keep in mind that you should be thankful for every moment you have and use them as tools. If everyone were to tap into the power of these gemstones, it would not only improve their lives, but it can be of incredible benefit to everyone around them as well.

CHAPTER 7
Healing Fundamentals

It is always important to remember that crystals possess a special kind of power. One that they harvested from the bowels of earth and time. Their unique energetic vibrations will have a direct impact on how you feel, think, and reason. So no matter what your intention, what you hope to accomplish, or whether you use a grid, a single crystal, or some other method, always select those stones that have properties that match your goals.

Choosing the right stone is one of the most important steps in crystal healing. Chances are, the first stones you choose will be based on their visual appeal. We can grow to understand that if you are being pulled towards that stone, it may not be solely based on your aesthetic preferences. While it may seem that way, you may subconsciously have connected to that stone's energy and recognize that it is the one that can provide you with what you need.

There are some people that are extremely sensitive to these vibrations of energy, but most are not. Still, as you get more in touch with a particular stone, even those who are not particularly sensitive to the vibrations will begin to notice small changes. So don't assume that because you are not highly sensitive to a particular stone, that it is not having some sort of effect on you. If you're unsure if a stone is working for you or not, try to exercise patience and recognize that the energy is there, and it is at work even if you don't see the results right away.

Keeping these thoughts in mind is extremely important for a beginner to crystal healing. It is easy to allow the naysayers of the world to dissuade you from this practice. The power in crystals is as real as your own willpower. All over the natural world, we respect the power of things we don't physically feel. The power of gravity, the electromagnetic waves, the mysterious force that moves the waves of the ocean. All of these things exert power and can affect us without us ever realizing it. The same is true of the crystals that come from the earth. Once you understand this basic fundamental, you are ready to embrace the power of crystals with an open mind and allow it to do its work on you. You are ready to establish your intentions.

Another important fundamental is your intention. Regardless of whether you're planning on using a single crystal or a grid, your purpose is the most important element in your healing process. Here, you must be completely honest with yourself, otherwise, your own inner desires will be working contrary to what you program your crystals to do. Some of the most common intentions for crystal healing are:

- Grounding yourself mentally, emotionally, or spiritually
- Finding love or repairing a damaged relationship
- Manifesting your dreams
- Healing old hurts and wounds
- Spiritual growth
- Practicing forgiveness or letting go of past wrongs
- Fertility, expanding your family

As you grow in your crystal healing knowledge, you'll likely find many more intentions that you can have and you will find the right stone for every one of them. However, honesty is the most important aspect of identifying these intentions and accessing their power.

For beginners, it might be best to start simply and grow from there. Most new ones start with three stones that have high vibrations to help you clear away your negative energies. Once these are cleared, you'll find it much easier to uncover more detailed intentions that you never knew you had.

Common starter stones are a piece of quartz to uplift and clear away negative energy that may be blocking you, obsidian to help you get grounded and activate your root chakra, and a blue kyanite to help you to open up and tune into all of your chakras so everything within you starts to work in better harmony.

Once you've got those fundamentals in order, you can move on to more specific approaches to crystal healing.

Chakra Healing

Every one of your chakras has a direct connection to specific colors, foods, sounds, smells, and crystals. Without even realizing it, many people are walking around in this chaotic world with our chakras unbalanced. This is pretty easy to do. Because our own personal energy field can be knocked off kilter by just about anything.

The good news is that it can be just as easily put back in place by using chakra healing crystals. When you use colored chakra crystals, you will get very specific vibrations that will help you to maintain balance and be able to cleanse your chakras at the same time. However, if you want to heal your chakras individually, here are a few suggestions that can put you on the right path and help you to choose the best crystal.

Healing the Root Chakra: Located right at the base of the spine, red-colored crystals work best on the root chakra. Look for crystals like smoky quartz, red garnet, hematite, red jasper, and black onyx. These will give you a solid grounding, a sense of security, and confidence to follow through on your goals.

Healing the Sacral Chakra: Located in the lower part of the abdomen, this chakra is best healed with orange-colored crystals. Your sacral chakra is out of balance when you are having problems with your sexuality, creativity, or personal power. Start off with crystals like amber, carnelian, goldstone, orange calcite or tiger's Eye.

Healing the Solar Plexus Chakra: Located right behind the navel, this chakra is the center of your breathing and is best healed with yellow-colored crystals. When the Solar Plexus is in balance you have more courage, honor, empathy, and a stronger connection with others. Look for stones like citrine, pyrite, rutilated quartz, and yellow jade.

Healing the Heart Chakra: Located in the center of the chest, the heart chakra has a powerful connection to the colors pink and green. When it is in balance you allow your heart to dictate the way you live. If it is blocked, you can open it with amazonite, aventurine, chrysoprase, emerald, green calcite, and rose quartz.

Healing the Throat Chakra: Located right about your collarbone in your throat, this chakra enhances your ability to communicate. It relies heavily on truthfulness and honesty in all things. It responds well to blue colored crystals like apatite, angelite, aquamarine, kyanite, and sodalite.

Healing the Third Eye Chakra: Located right in the middle of the forehead right between the eyebrows, your third eye enhances your intuition, guidance, and self-realization. It responds well to the color purple so choose stones of amethyst, angelite, charoite, flourite, and iolite.

Healing the Crown Chakra: Located right at the top of your head, this chakra is very good at distributing energy throughout the body. It is more closely connected to your spirituality, meditation, and helps you to think deeply about matters. It responds well to the color white so look for stones like amethyst, blue lace agate, ametrine, clear quartz, and lepidolite.

As you can probably tell, some of the crystals mentioned here can be used for more than one chakra, so don't feel like they can't be used for other intentions once your original purpose has been fulfilled. However, just by matching the color of the crystal with the chakra you want to unblock you can open yourself up to a whole new world of positive experiences.

Energy Healing

Every part of your body has its own energy vibration. Every stone has its own energy vibration. The goal of crystal healing is to match the stone to the energy source that you are lacking so it can infuse more energy where you need it most. In the above section, we spoke about which chakras help you in what areas and which stones will yield the best results. Once you've chosen your stone, then you have to know how to use them in the right way.

There are more than a few ways to work with crystals, but here are just a few basic steps that will apply in nearly every situation.

Use the crystal while meditating: Meditation and crystal healing are natural partners. It is a means of combining the energy of the crystal with the mind, body, and spirit all at the same time. When you meditate, hold the crystal in both hands, close your eyes, and focus only on your breathing. As you do, you will notice that your body will feel like it is being pulled down to the earth. Don't worry about this, it is the crystal working to ground you. The longer you meditate, the lighter you should begin to feel.

For beginners, you may not feel anything the first few times you try it. There are some crystals that just doesn't have a strong enough vibration to give you the sensations you're looking for, but that doesn't mean they are not working. Each crystal will feel different to you, so be patient. If after a time, you still do not feel the changes you're looking for, try a different crystal. The key is to be patient and to be open enough to allow the power of the crystal to come in.

Crystal Grids: One of the best ways to restore energy to the body is through a crystal grid. When using your grid, always choose those stones that are closely aligned with your intentions and use a grid along with sacred geometry. The power of the crystals working together will help to manifest your intentions to the universe and draw in the energy you seek.

Some people also like to incorporate a bit of Feng Shui in their crystal grids to help them to choose the right colors and location to place the grid in order to get the best results.

Designate a crystal space: By designating a space for your crystals, you can attract more energy to you. This is a common practice that is often used in yoga and meditation. When your crystals have a permanent home where they can be displayed in all their glory, they can serve as a constant reminder to you to connect with your intention frequently. Any time you enter into your inner sanctum, just the vision of their calming display not only will add a touch of beauty to your life but an inner peace along with it.

One of the most popular crystals for a sacred space of this nature is the amethyst. It sends out a constant stream of positive energy and helps you to achieve a deeper state of meditation. You can also place crystal points in your space to strengthen your intention and amplify your goals.

Wear or carry your crystals: Many people have smaller crystals that they carry around with them wherever they go. Smaller crystals allow you to have more contact with them as you can touch them whenever you need to. You can have them made on a keychain, carry them in your pocket or in your handbag so that you have access to it whenever you want. It can serve as a reminder that you have an ultimate purpose that you are working towards and keep you from getting distracted.

Position crystals on your body: Placing crystals on your body will give you a completely different effect than you get by simply holding them in your hand. If you're trying to heal a specific chakra, place the crystal directly on the chakra. It will stir up the energy emanating from that chakra and draw out the emotions that you need to address in order to heal.

Combine crystals with yoga practice: Another very effective way of using crystals is to place them around your yoga mat while you practice your positions. This will help you to achieve a more tranquil state of mind and encourage an even deeper state of healing while meditating.

Use them as decorations: In addition to their healing properties, crystals also create a nice aesthetic addition to your home décor. Larger crystals especially those that make for great conversation pieces can do quite well in shifting the energy in your space to a more positive one. For example, a large piece of amethyst can create positive vibes and push out any negative energy that may enter the room, making for a consistently peaceful environment.

Use crystals in your bath: We all know just how soothing a soak in a hot bath can be. Using crystals and essential oils can only enhance those benefits even more. Let them soak in the water with you so that they can restore any energy you've lost after a long stressful day. If you don't have time to soak in a bath, then soak your crystals in warm water before you wash your face, to give you a little bit of peace and calm before you start your day.

Reiki Healing

Reiki Healing is an alternative form of energy healing that comes from Japan. It involves transferring universal energy from one person to the next. Unlike with crystal energy, it is the transferring of this energy through the laying on of hands and can be used to treat a wide number of psychological and emotional states of mind. While there is not a lot of research done to date on Reiki, many believe that it can be used to relieve pain and treat a number of other physical ailments.

The word "Reiki" literally can be translated to mean "mysterious atmosphere" and it is most commonly used to target the energy fields that surround the body. In the case of physical pain, the idea is that when there is an injury of some kind, the energy can get stuck in that place and eventually stagnate to the point that there is not just physical pain but emotional pain as well.

Reiki can be used to unblock the energy that flows through that injured area. Like every other form of energy healing, Reiki works on improving the flow of energy in the body's aura, so that you are better able to relax, reduce the pain, and escalate the healing process.

To enhance the benefits of Reiki healing, using them together with crystals will help to improve the recovery process even faster.

There are several different ways you can use Reiki in this way. Some Reiki Masters prefer to use the Tibetan Master symbol, which can be drawn over the crystal. The user then repeats the name of the symbol three times in order to activate it. Then in their mind, they visualize the symbol as it passes right through the crystal, cleaning away any negative energy as it does.

If you're inclined to work with symbols like this, then you can practice programming the crystal to go a step further and physically heal and give you grounding at the same time. For a more physical healing, you can use the Cho-Ku-Rei symbol to help you. If the healing is more of an emotional nature, then use the Se-He-Ki to give you more stability.

Reiki can also be used in a more intuitive way. By drawing the Reiki down from the Crown Chakra all the way to the arms crossing it over into the hands, you can ask the crystal to help heal any individual you have in mind. Simply focus your mind on that person and ask the crystal to work its magic.

Reiki Kotodama: For those who have advanced enough to get past using symbols, you can graduate to using Reiki Kotodama. This is the process of chanting specific sacred sounds in order to evoke a change in the energy and vibrations of the crystals. As you chant, the crystals you hold in your hand will start to vibrate differently, which can not only affect you but also the environment. The Kotodama is an ancient Japanese form of chanting that teaches that every vowel chanted has its own mystical powers and vibrations. So when you connect with the crystal using these chants, the crystal will emit a very specific form of energy that can alter the person, object, or the surrounding environment in the way it is intended.

Spiritual Healing

More and more people are accepting the fact that there is a spiritual being inside of them. In fact, there is a direct connection between one's spirituality and their physical health. Using crystals can help you to connect better to the spiritual person buried deep inside of you. Anyone who is interested in tapping into the spiritual gifts we all possess, then crystals are the way to access them.

There are many crystals that can aid you on your spiritual journey. Since crystals are gaining in popularity now, they can easily be obtained without having to spend a lot of time searching them out.

Because of this, more people are using them now and getting in touch with their more spiritual side.

If you are unfamiliar with the connection between spirituality and physical health, then you're likely not sure what kind of healing these can provide. Many people suffer from emotional issues and how they can be healed through their own spirituality. However, using heart chakra stones can be a good way to get started and learn at the same time.

Whether you're trying to heal a broken heart, nurture an inner child, or deal with some other issue, it is just a matter of choosing the right crystals to work with. Many metaphysical healers are now using crystals in their practices to aid people to find their spiritual path. They not only create a connection to all of the beings inside of you (physical, emotional, spiritual), but they also are very effective in easing many of the health issues that people may face.

Anyone who wants to benefit in a spiritual way can do so with the right stones. For spiritual healing, start with a piece of green fuchsite. Take it to your healing space and start with a meditation practice while holding it. It will help you to open up to others in your life and give you the freedom to live your own life the way you want.

Meditation is the secret to making this type of healing work. Regardless of the type of meditation you use, it can open up your chakras in a way that allows you to get into contact with your higher spiritual being.

For beginners, learning how to meditate is not always easy so it is probably best to start with short sessions that can grow in length over time. While there are many variations of meditation, if you follow the basics, you can get started pretty quickly. After you've mastered these skills, you can then move on to other meditation techniques that you can apply. If one meditation form doesn't work for you, keep searching, you'll find one that matches you perfectly.

- Find a location where you can sit comfortably. Some people like to sit on the floor while others prefer to sit on a chair. Your position should be a place where you can sit upright, but still have a relaxed position. You want to be reasonably comfortable but not too comfortable.

- If you like, you can put on some music, but make sure that it is more relaxing. You might even want to purchase a little meditation mood music to help you get your mind in the right place.

- Close your eyes and start taking in slow, deep breaths, concentrating on the flow of air going in and out. This will help you to relax even more. Notice how your body feels more relaxed after each breath.

- As you continue this slow, rhythmic breathing, allow your consciousness to start focusing on your toes.
- Tense your toes and then your legs, then release the tension and fall into a relaxed position again. Feel the tension as it leaves your body, making you feel even more relaxed.

- Continue this exercise, tensing and relaxing each part of the body until you get up to the top of your head.

- Imagine a light hovering just above it.

- Focus on that light and allow it to travel down into your body.

- As it travels, allow the tension to be released from each part of the body the light touches.

- Allow the light to go down and stop at your third eye, then down your throat, and keep doing this through all of your chakras.

- Finally, allow the light to leave your body through your root chakra and enter back into the earth pulling you along with it. This will ground you and your energy to the earth, letting you connect to the natural elements that surround you.

- Allow the light to grow outwards creating a bubble of light that surrounds you.

- Stay within this light for as long as you want.

- Take the time to sit in this relaxed state and let your mind drift and soak in all of its spiritual essences allowing it to flood your entire body.

Regular practice of this type of meditation, especially done while holding crystals in your hands will help to clear away any disharmony inside of you. When you have drunk your fill of this light, say a quiet "Thank you" to the spirit, allow the light to go from you and embrace in the excess energy you have acquired.

This type of meditation is very easy to do. You don't need to memorize any special chants or use any unique equipment or tools. All you need is your body and a few crystals to hold and you're all set.

To do this, though, you need to have some grounding crystals. This will help you to connect better with the light and help you to ground yourself more easily to nature. The best crystals for this are the smoky quartz, black obsidian, shamanite, black calcite, and black tourmaline. Connecting to your spiritual self can be extremely rewarding as long as you choose the right crystals to work with. Start simply and grow with the process as you gain more knowledge and you'll be well on your way to making a spiritual connection that will take you into a whole new realm of what's possible.

CHAPTER 8
How To Choose The Right Crystals

There are many different ways to choose crystals. We've already discussed the fact that the crystals are actually the ones making the choice in your partnership, but it is still your responsibility to know when they are calling to you.

In order to choose correctly, you need to be very familiar with the condition you are trying to heal. Knowing your intention will help steer you in the right direction and allow the crystal to be able to pick up on your vibes.

You can also choose your crystals by the way they appear to you. Crystals usually first draw people in because of their intrinsic natural beauty and striking colors. It is only after this initial pull that you begin to notice the other features of a true crystal.

Sometimes crystals find their way to you through no act of your own. You may receive one as a gift or you may discover one someplace near your home.

However way the crystal comes into your possession, follow your intuition. It is the best way to know for sure if the crystal is the right fit for your purposes. You may not realize it, but you already are gifted with the natural instinct to make this choice.

When you are drawn to a particular crystal, allow it to pull you in. Pick it up and hold it in the palm of your hand. Close your eyes and focus all of your energy on feeling the vibration and allow it to connect with your own inner vibrations. As you hold it, don't be surprised if you start to see images in your mind's eye. You may see a splash of color if you are strongly connected to it. If the crystal is not the right crystal for you, you will know it. You'll have a strong sense that something is not adding up or you won't be able to connect with its vibrations.

There is a unique kind of mystery that surrounds crystals that you have chosen. We recognize their energy, but often do not understand it fully. It is said that crystals will only remain with you as long as you need their energy. Many people usually report that their crystals have suddenly disappeared after they have fulfilled their purpose. It is like they have returned back to the earth from where they have come. So don't be surprised to find your crystal missing after you've used it for a while. This is a good sign that you've healed and your purpose is fulfilled, or that you now have a new purpose that another crystal may be better suited for.

Where to Buy Crystals

There are three ways to buy your crystals. Many people choose to buy them through online sites as they can be much cheaper than walking into a brick and mortar shop to purchase some rare form brought in from some distant region of the world.

However, buying online has its own drawbacks. One of the most important keys to choosing the right crystal is making a physical connection with it. Buying them online prevents you from doing this. In addition, there is no way you can determine the true authenticity of a stone without having the chance to examine it carefully.

This does not mean that all online dealers are deceptive. There are many dealers that produce crystals of a very high quality from online shops, and there are many individuals who are extremely intuitive and can choose a perfect crystal match just from looking at an image on their computer screen. In time, you will gain that kind of skill and talent, but for purchasing your first crystal, it is probably best to take a more tactile approach to select one that will work well for you.

Another way to purchase crystals is to visit events and shows. In fact, this is an excellent way to find unique crystals that have unusual shapes and patterns. When buying these types of crystals, keep in mind that you will be purchasing something that may have been handled by hundreds or even thousands of people before it finds its way to you. This can affect the kind of energy they emit so you may need to spend a little more time connecting with it before you make a decision.

Finally, you can purchase them through a brick and mortar shop. There are many specialty shops that deliver high-quality crystals on a more personal level. These are probably the best option for the beginner as the owners or workers in these shops have specialized knowledge that can help to guide you in making the right choice. They also allow you to closely inspect the stones and spend more time with it, so you can be sure that you're choosing the best one for you.

Choosing Crystal Shapes

You also want to pay close attention to the shape of the crystal you choose. While the healing properties within the crystal will remain constant regardless of the shape, the experience you have when connecting with it may differ because of it. There are many facets of crystal shapes you should be aware of that will help you to decide exactly which shape will work best for your needs.

The Point: Crystal points are those crystals that have intense energy and can channel or amplify it in many ways. You can use a crystal point to focus the energy inward when the point is facing you or outward by focusing it away. Points are one of the best starter crystals because their energy can be easily harnessed and directed to where you want it to go.

The Cube: Crystal cubes are often used when working with the root chakra. It is an excellent grounding stone that can bring in a powerful sense of calm to your environment. Cubes can also help you to create a protective grid surrounding your environment by placing one in each corner of your space.

The Pyramid: The pyramid is considered to be one of the sacred shapes used throughout many ancient civilizations. When you want to send out a concentrated beam of energy into the universe or make your intentions manifest, you would use the crystal pyramid by setting it on top of the paper you have written them on.

The Heart: The heart-shaped crystal is used as a reminder that you need to continue to use the healing properties and keep them close. People work with them as a form of spiritual nourishment that will help them to always give and accept energy sent out to them.

The Harmonizer: These cylinder-shaped crystals help you with meditation and make it easier for you to enter a more spiritually stimulated space. They also help with giving you a better sense of mental and physical balance.

The Cluster: Crystal clusters are some of the most beautiful creations found in nature. A cluster occurs only when you have many points that develop within the same matrix. Clusters generally vibrate at a higher energy so having one in your sacred space will keep your energy levels high, so you have more power to work with.

Tumbled Stones: These stones can be used in a variety of ways. Those that are small with smooth surfaces can be carried in your pocket or purse. They are perfect pieces to make into jewelry and they are ideal of use in a crystal grid. They also make great starter stones because they are easy to use and draw energy from.

What to Look For

Knowing exactly what to look for in a crystal is extremely important as it is the one decision that will start you on your journey to balancing your energy and healing yourself. When it comes to buying these little gems, you want to be absolutely sure that you're getting the kind of quality you need. If you are intuitive enough to pick out a quality piece of crystal, you've saved yourself from a whole lot of headaches.

You can also look at the color of the crystal. There is no doubt that each color has its own healing properties. For a detailed list of each color and their healing properties, you can refer to a crystal directory. These have a color and an image of each crystal categorized by its healing properties. However, below is a list of the most common colors and what they can do.

Black: Power, protection, and mystery. Black obsidian, black tourmaline, hematite, jet, and onyx are the most common black crystals used.

Blue: Tranquility and emotional healing. Angelite, aquamarine, apatite, blue lace agate, azurite, blue chalcedony, celestine, and chrysocolla.

Brown: Absorb negative energy and harness the healing powers of the earth. Smoky quartz, brown jasper, bronzite, tiger's eye, and petrified wood.

Yellow/Gold: From the color of the sun, these stones give optimism and joy. Amber, citrine, golden topaz, yellow tiger's eye, pyrite, and yellow jasper.

Green: Activates the heart chakra and provides an emotional balance. Brings good fortune and prosperity. Aventurine, emerald, green fluorite, jade, and malachite.

Orange: Arouse passion in the spirit. Captures the spirit and energy from the sun. aragonite, calcite, copper, carnelian, and sunstone.

Pink: Love and compassion, heart energizers, and opens up the heart. Pink tourmaline, pink sapphire, rose quartz, and lepidolite.

Grey: Reflects the moonlight and the expanse of the universe. Provides protective shield. Hematite and moonstone.

Purple: Gives enlightenment and intuition. They keep emotions balanced and provide relaxing and soothing vibes. They can also amplify the energy, especially when used with the heart chakra. Amethyst and charoite.

Red: Infuses passion and has a grounding energy that supports the root chakra. Garnet, ruby, and red tiger's eye.

White: Represents purity and transformation. Excellent healing tools when used with other healing grids. Clear quartz and selenite.

You can also look for stones based on the chakra you want to heal.

Crown Chakra: Selenite and clear quartz

The Third Eye: Lapis lazuli, sodalite, and fluorite

The Throat Chakra: Aquamarine, angelite, blue apatite, sodalite

The Heart Chakra: Aventurine and rhodonite

Solar Plexus Chakra: Pyrite, rutilated quartz, citrine, and yellow jasper

Sacral Chakra: Carnelian, orange calcite, tiger's eye, and sunstone.

Root Chakra: Black onyx, red garnet, red jasper, hematite, and smoky quartz.

There are many ways to look for the right crystal for you. If you're still not sure, don't be shy about asking the shopkeeper to assist you. They work with these stones every day and have a highly trained intuitiveness that helps them match you with the right crystal.

What to Avoid

Buying crystals can be a little scary at first. You walk into a nice little shop and you may see hundreds of crystals on display. Unlike heading into your local supermarket where all produce is placed together and the deli counter has all the cuts you want, crystal shop owners do not have such a regimented way to display their wares. It is left entirely up to the individual owners so what may work for you in one shop may not be the same at the next shop.

This makes it hard to walk into the store and quickly find exactly what you're looking for. So don't hesitate to browse and ask questions. Still, while crystal healing is a noble occupation, it doesn't mean that all the shop owners are equally as noble. There are some major pitfalls you will want to be aware of.

Natural or Manmade: Now that modern science has been able to imitate the creation of a crystal in the laboratory, synthetic crystals should cost far less than natural ones. Examine the crystal closely looking for flaws. If it seems too perfect with no flaws, it's a good chance it is manmade and it won't bring you the same kind of power that comes from those crystals that have been shaped by millions of years in the earth.

Labels: You also want to keep a close eye out for stones with a trademark name or that comes with an excessively high price tag. Any name that is trademarked may be the same quality as one that is not, but they will cost a great deal more.

Check for Alternations: Some crystals may have been altered from their natural state. This may also alter the effectiveness of the crystal. Some shop owners may change the appearance of a crystal so that it looks more like another crystal. They may dye it, heat it, or coat it so that it appears to be another stone with completely different properties.

There are many ways you can "fake" a crystal. It may have started out as a partially real crystal but when you coat the exterior or combine it with a synthetic, like what is often done with opals and turquoise, you may find yourself buying mostly glass. Rubies are another crystal that is often altered in some way.

To determine if it's a fake, you can ask the seller, but if it is, he's not likely going to tell you. However, there are a few other steps you can take to be sure.

1. Check the base for any signs of mounting, glue, or paint.
2. Look for uneven coloring or shades not normally found in nature.
3. Look into the glass for signs of air bubbles

4. Look for flaws. All naturally occurring crystals have flaws. If it looks too perfect, chances are, it is.

While there may be many crystals that can be altered in some form, there are some common crystals that you should be watchful of. Since finding authentic turquoise is rare, it can be quite expensive. Sellers will usually make a synthetic stone that is made from dyed resin or ceramic. They may also substitute it with howlite, which has veins that are very similar to turquoise veins. You can identify fake turquoise quite easily. First, its blue color will appear to be unnatural and there will be brown lines running through it.

Another crystal to be cautious of is citrine. Most of what you will see in a crystal shop is not authentic citrine, but in fact, amethyst which has been heat-treated until it turns to the desired yellow color. The heat will actually change the properties of the stone, so it is always important to get some sort of authentication before you make a purchase.

CHAPTER 9
Crystals And What Ails You

At the core of every crystal healing is the desire to infuse your life with something that will bring about a positive change. However, there are thousands of ways you can accomplish that with crystals, so before you can decide on which form of crystal healing you want, you need to carefully examine and get a more precise idea of what type of remedy you need.

The remedies that follow are not meant as a cure-all for the issues they address but are only given as a possible alternative form of treatment to consider. Your particular issues may be successfully dealt with using these methods or you may opt to use them in conjunction with a medical and psychological treatment at the same time. However, using crystals, whether alone or alongside other traditional forms of treatment, can add a powerful element to your life, so they are definitely worth giving them some serious consideration.

Abandonment

There are many people who may not even realize that they have issues with feelings of abandonment. These can stem from a loss that happened years earlier and may not even seem related to the challenges that they face today. Suffering from a past break-up or even a loss of a loved one can leave them feeling empty and alone.

Using a chant or a mantra to remind you that finding unconditional love is something that is found when one first loves themselves. Chanting along with crystals can edify you both spiritually and emotionally and give you the kind of support you need when things are the most difficult.

One crystal that works well with Abandonment issues is the rose quartz. When using it along with deep meditation and visualization, you will gradually begin to feel its warm effects.

- Hold the rose quartz in your hands.
- Visualize yourself enveloped in its warm, pink light while focusing on your breathing.
- Continue this visualization for a minimum of 10 minutes and maintain it until you start to feel a calming sense of peace.

You can expand this form of healing even further by setting up a crystal grid and placing it close to where you work or sleep. Use the rose quartz as the center stone and place a square of apache tears, amazonite, carnelian, and garnet around it. Each of these stones will bring a different element to your healing.

Rose quartz will bring unconditional love
Apache tears will help to release the grief
Amazonite will heal the emotional pain
Carnelian will empower you
And Garnet will give you a stronger sense of belonging

Together, these stones can offer the kind of healing that will rejuvenate you and put you on a more stable grounding.

A second way to heal abandonment issues is by combining rose quartz with citrine & obsidian chakra work. Start by lying on your back in a comfortable position. Place the rose quartz on your heart chakra. Then place the citrine crystal on your solar plexus chakra and the obsidian on your root chakra.

Close your eyes and start to breathe deeply, repeating the following chant until you start to feel a calming sense of peace.

Affirmation: *I give myself unconditional love and will accept unconditional love from the universe.*

When dealing with abandonment issues, it helps to uncover why you are having these negative feelings. If you're not really sure of the reason behind it, start with some mindfulness practice. It will help you to uncover your true source of the problem so that you can target your healing more accurately.

Abuse

The psychological damage that results from abuse can be astronomical, and its effects can negatively impact your life for years, leaving many scars. Struggling to overcome this damage on your own can sometimes seem impossible.

Each type of abuse can have its own unique signature in the different chakras. A person dealing with sexual abuse may have a blockage in their root chakra, while someone dealing with abuse from their parents may have a blockage in their solar plexus or sacral chakras. Because abuse can be so varied, it might be best to seek out psychological counseling and use the crystal healing treatments as an additional support to help you heal faster from the trauma.

Affirmation: *I release the pain and hurt from my past in exchange for a more positive and loving future.*

The Meditation: Start by closing your eyes and allowing the pain and suffering you felt in the past to come in. Take notice of where you feel that pain. Take a few deep inhalations and start to visualize the light from the crystal entering your body through your breath. Allow it to fill you up and flow to where you feel the pain. As you exhale, repeat the affirmation. Continue in this exercise until you start to feel a sense of calm come over you.

Depending on how severe your trauma has been, you may not feel results right away. If you don't feel anything during the first few sessions, continue the exercise for at least ten minutes and repeat it regularly until you start to sense the positive energy entering you.

Garnet: As you go through your meditation, you can use the garnet on your root chakra. It will help you to release all the pain of your past and reclaim your own power. As a support to the meditation, you can also keep a garnet with you wherever you go, to keep a cloud of calm positive energy around you at all times.

Abuse can affect several chakras at the same time, so always place the crystals on the damaged chakras to help clear away any energy blocks. Below are some suggestions, but feel free to use any crystals that will help heal the pain in any of your blocked chakras.

Garnet: root chakra
Carnelian: sacral chakra
Yellow tiger's eye: solar plexus chakra
Rose quartz: heart chakra
Lapis lazuli: throat chakra

It is important to understand that rather than trying to suppress the pain you feel from the abuse, these treatments work better if you acknowledge them. Suppressing pain can often make it worse by forcing it deeper down into your soul making it even harder to recover. When you recognize that you have pain, it is the first step in letting it go, so you can move on with your life.

Acceptance

Sometimes our struggles are because we can't let go of regrets or painful past memories. We spend all of our days reliving things that can't be changed or consumed with excessive worry about the future. This often keeps us from living in the present moment, the only time period that we have control over.

When difficult things arise, we need to learn how to accept those things. If this has not been your habit, it can be difficult to do. It means surrendering to what has happened and no longer allowing it to have control over us. For many, that is a huge change in their thinking.

Affirmation: *I accept things as they are and release from my hold anything that is not in my power to change.*

Meditation:

- Find a comfortable sitting position
- Close your eyes and focus on your feelings
- Take note of where in your body the pain presents itself

- Repeat the affirmation
- Visualize the pain as a black mass
- Take note of the white light that enters your body as you breathe
- Watch the light cause the mass to slowly begin to dissolve
- Exhale slowly, letting the dissolution leave your body with each exhale
- Continue this practice for a least ten minutes or until you begin to feel a sense of calm.

Crystals: There are several crystals that will enhance the effects of the meditation to help you let go of this negativity that consumes you.

Apatite: This is the stone of acceptance. Keep it close to your heart. You can wear it as a necklace or a pendant around your neck.

Apache tears: These small stones help bring relief from disappointment and make it easier for you to accept things that make you uncomfortable. Hold them in your hand as you repeat the Serenity Prayer.

God grant me the serenity to accept the things I cannot change, the courage to change the things I can, and the wisdom to know the difference.

Part of the reason people struggle with letting go is society's idea that to surrender means that you are weak, but in reality, it is a sign of true strength. Allowing yourself to accept that some things are completely out of your control can empower you to take positive steps towards those things you can handle, giving you better prospects of a brighter future.

Addiction

Addiction does not always have to be to some illegal substance or alcohol. You can be addicted to your favorite food, an activity or sport, or something else entirely. The problem with addiction is that once it gets out of control, it can disrupt your life in some very extreme ways. One way to treat this type of addiction is with psychological therapy. However, crystals can help you on a higher plane by giving you spiritual grounding and emotional stability that will empower you so you can resist the constant pull of your addiction.

Affirmation: *I am free of my desires for _____ and I set them free, releasing me from their hold.*
Meditation: When you are addicted, you have an imbalance in all of your chakras. Practicing meditation with crystals placed on all of your chakras is a great way to restore balance. You can work with one chakra at a time or you can choose to work with them one by one. The two main chakras you should start with are the sacral chakra and the throat chakra. These two are directly linked to your willpower and can help you gain better control of your addiction.

- Lie in a comfortable position
- Close your eyes and concentrate on your breathing
- Place crystals on one or all of your chakras
- As you exhale on each breath, repeat the serenity prayer out loud
- Continue with this exercise for at least 10 minutes or until you can feel the energy of the crystals empower you.

Labradorite: Carry it with you or wear it throughout your day. Make sure it is close to you when your cravings are the strongest. Labradorite helps to detoxify your body and free you from the effects of your addition.

You can also sleep with it underneath your pillow. You must clean your labradorite daily, so it is free from the energy that is commonly associated with addiction.

Amethyst: Sometimes referred to as the sober stone. You can wear it as jewelry or carry it around with you as you go about your daily routine. It can be especially helpful when you find you are going through withdrawal symptoms.

You can also create a crystal grid using the sacred geometry that gives you more power. These will only reinforce the therapy you're likely already getting to deal with your addiction issues.

It is important to understand that addiction usually is triggered by underlying issues from your past that hasn't been addressed yet. Often, the addiction is not the real problem but only a symptom for something else in your past. As you work through crystal healing your addictions, consider also doing a deep introspective study to see if you can uncover the true source of your addiction.

Anger

There is both good anger and bad anger. It is a perfectly normal emotion when it is controlled. Healthy anger can enter our body, express itself, and quickly dissipate without leaving any harm behind. However, when we are demonstrating an unhealthy form of this emotion, it can turn ugly very quickly. Unresolved anger can slowly fester like an open wound and turn into resentment, causing a domino effect that will lead to other problems in your life. Learning how to let go of your anger will help you to move on to a more positive a healthy emotional life.

Affirmation: *I breathe in the peace that surrounds me and releases the anger in return.*

Meditation:

- Find a comfortable sitting position
- Place both hands over the solar plexus chakra
- Breathe in slowly
- As you inhale, visualize the peace filling you up and flowing throughout your body.
- Say the affirmation as you slowly exhale
- Imagine your anger leaving you through your nose
- Repeat this exercise for at least 10 minutes or until you feel the peace enter into you

Anxiety

Anxiety is another very normal emotion that we all feel. Under normal circumstances, your anxiety can be heightened at times and then can stabilize allowing you to continue on living the best life you can. However, when a person is found to be in a heightened state of anxiety, it can cause both physical and emotional damage.

Anxiety has many faces, it doesn't always appear the same in every situation, nor in every person. Extreme anxiety can present itself as phobias, obsessive-compulsive disorder, or PTSD. Milder cases could be seen as a social phobia, nervousness, and avoidance techniques. Anxiety is closely connected to the root chakra as it relates to a strong sense of security, so crystal therapy with this chakra can help to ease some of the pressures and make you feel more confident.

Affirmation: *I relax in infinite serenity.*

Meditation:

- Find a comfortable sitting position
- Hold your crystal in your hands
- Close your eyes and take deep breaths
- With each inhale, visualize the peace entering your body with it
- Repeat the affirmation
- As you exhale, visualize the anxiety leaving with each breath
- Repeat for at least 10 minutes or until you feel the anxiety begin to subside

Crystals

Blue lace agate: Its peaceful blue color has a calming effect. Wear it or carry it with you, especially when you are expecting to be in stressful situations.
Lapis lazuli & and clear quartz grid: Here is where a grid can be extremely helpful. With a circular grid, use a large lapis lazuli

for its focus stone. Around it, place eight clear quartz points in a circle. Make sure to turn the quartz points away from the lapis lazuli so that they are directed outward. This will amplify the calming qualities in the environment, giving you a strong sense of peace.

Black tourmaline: Carry it around with you when you are feeling anxious. This is a grounding stone that will absorb much of your negativity.

Boundaries

Setting boundaries can be difficult for some people. To be able to do this, one needs to understand their own limitations. With this understanding, they can then help others to understand how they should be treated.

At times, setting boundaries is hard because we all want people to like us. It can be difficult to think that you are going against the grain and so we are reluctant to demand the respect we know we deserve, creating an internal conflict within us.

Affirmation: *I can assert my wishes in kindness, confidence, and compassion.*

Meditation: Your solar plexus chakra is at the very heart of your self-identity. Without balance in this area, it can be difficult to know how to set boundaries. Your throat chakra is where you communicate those boundaries, so you need to activate both of these chakras in your meditation practice.

- Lie down on your back
- Close your eyes and concentrate on your solar plexus chakra
- Inhale deeply
- Ask "what are my boundaries"
- Lie still, breathing normally while you meditate on this question
- Keep your focus on your solar plexus

- Slowly slide your hand up your midline and let it rest on your throat chakra
- Repeat the same affirmation 10 times or until your boundaries are revealed to you

Crystals: As you are trying to determine your boundaries, place a citrine crystal underneath your pillow. Repeat the same question as you are drifting off to sleep so that it can help you to understand. When you wake the next morning, write down what was revealed for you. Repeat this process every night for a week and your boundaries will then become clear.

After you have identified your boundaries, you can use a rose quartz to give you compassion and sodalite to help you with communicating these to others. Carrying these two crystals around with you will help you to better assert yourself in a kind and compassionate way whenever you need to.

Centering

The act of calming the mind, body, and spirit can aid you in many ways. When a person is centered, they are not just calm and relaxed, but they are also more alert. This makes it easy for the energy to flow in and out of them and allows them to tap into their own creativity. Centered people are more in tune with their feelings and have a strong intuition that can help them to communicate better with the spirit world.

Affirmation: *I relax my body, mind, and spirit so I can find my center.*

Meditation:

- Find a comfortable sitting position
- Sit with your eyes closed
- Breathe in deeply
- As you breathe, take notice of how the breathing is relaxing you

- Focus your mind on your center (this is the point between your solar plexus and sacral chakras)
- Concentrate on this area as you let the breathing bring you to a calmer state

Crystals: Blue lace agate is an excellent calming crystal that can help you find your center. Hold the stone in one hand while you are meditating. Breathe in deeply and let its calm cover you. You can also make it a habit of carrying the blue lace agate stone with you wherever you go. Pull it out whenever you find you are feeling a little off center, so it can help you to find your way.

Clear quartz is a crystal you can reach for at the start of every day. This one can also be used during meditation.

- Sit in a comfortable position
- Hold a piece of clear quartz in your non-dominant hand
- Close your eyes and take in 10 deep breaths
- Focus on your core
- Feel the energy from the crystal enter your body
- It will naturally gravitate towards your center

Change

Whether you are accepting or giving change, it can be very difficult to handle. This is likely because we instinctively fear the unknown. However, life would never exist without change so being able to accept it and adapt to it is crucial to our survival.

Affirmation for Accepting Change: *I am thankful for the changes I have experienced because they give me the power to grow.*

Affirmation for Creating Change: *I am motivated to make the necessary changes in my life because I know I need them to grow.*

Meditation:

- Find a quiet place and sit in a comfortable position
- Close your eyes

- Place both of your hands over your heart chakra
- Take a few deep breaths
- Visualize the fluid white energy floating down through your crown chakra and flooding your body
- Let it fill up your arms and hands before going into the heart chakra
- Repeat the affirmation for at least 10 minutes or until you feel the peace and comfort to accept the change.

Crystals: When you are going through a period of extreme change, carry a piece of watermelon tourmaline with you. It will give you the kind of calmness you need to be able to accept and understand the new situation.

The prehnite & clear quartz grid can also be very effective. Use the prehnite as your Focus stone and three clear quartz points form a triangle around it. Make sure the points are facing outward away from the center of the grid. The points will help to amplify the power of the prehnite and bring you the kind of strength you need to accept what's coming.

There may be times when you are reluctant to accept the change in your life and continue on doing the same routine even though it is not working for you. It can be difficult to take the necessary steps that will move you in the right direction. Your comfort zone is where you live and you can't seem to move from it. In such cases, your meditation will take on a different kind of tone.

- Find a comfortable sitting position
- Sit with your eyes closed and your body relaxed
- Relax your mind
- Visualize where you feel you need to make changes in your life
- Allow yourself to go through the change in your mind's eye
- Follow through on your mental actions until the change comes to a logical conclusion
- Reward yourself with joy and positive energy from making the change

- Repeat the chat for nine more times. (In Numerology, nine is the number for completion)

Crystals: Blue or green aventurine. These opportunity stones are open to change. Start by sleeping with this stone under your pillow to work on your subconscious mind while you sleep. It will subtly awaken your desire for change.

Blue kyanite is used to break free from many old habits that may cause you to get into a rut. When meditating, hold the blue kyanite in your non-dominant hand. As you take each breath, repeat the chant for bringing change into your life, and as you exhale, release those old habits into the universe.

Start trying to think of change in a different way. Instead of thinking of it as something you have no choice over, reframe your thinking to accept that change as another way of introducing new opportunities into your life.

Cleansing

Cleansing is another element of life that can make people uncomfortable. When you cleanse, you push out your negativity and make room for more positive vibes to enter your world. Cleansing does not limit itself to a spiritual cleanse, you can also apply this when you move into a new home, enter a new relationship, or embrace a whole new space in your life. Cleansing crystals can also be used when you are trying to push out negativity from something bad that might have happened (a fight with a loved one, a serious illness, or a tragedy of some sort).

Affirmation: *This space is filled with the light of love*

Meditation:

- Position yourself in a seating position in the center of the space you want to be cleansed
- Close your eyes and breathe normally

- Visualize the white light descending from above and enveloping you
- Allow the light to push out all energy in the space
- Repeat the chat for ten full minutes or until you sense that the space has been cleansed

Crystals: When cleansing a physical space, place a clear quartz cluster in the center of the area. You can also place smaller pieces of it around the perimeter of the room. Stand in the center with your eyes closed. From this position, start your meditation practice.

Black tourmaline can be used after smudging. Smudging is when you light a bunch of sage, cedar, sweetgrass, or lavender. Once it is lit, blow out the flame and let the smoke tendrils waft in the air. Moving in a clockwise direction, carry the smoking herbs around the perimeter of the room and wave it around every entrance. Visualize the white light entering the room and repeat the affirmation again.

Once you have completed the smudging around the entire space, take four pieces of black tourmaline and place one in each of the four corners of the space to ward off any new negative energy that may enter the room later.

For emotional cleansing, you need to enter a physical cleaning first by bathing. Using some simple techniques, you can remove any type of lingering negativity, so you can feel a new spirit enter you. One should go through cleansing anytime they have gone through a difficult negative period or when you feel like you need to be refreshed for some reason.

Affirmation: *I am filling myself with pure cleaning white light*

Meditation:

- Sit in a comfortable position
- Close your eyes
- Visualize the white light entering your body from above
- Allow it to travel down through you passing through each chakra until it touches the earth

- Repeat this meditation practice for about 10 minutes anytime you feel the need for emotional cleansing

Crystals: Start by dissolving a quarter cup of Himalayan Pink Salt in the bathtub. Sit in the tub and let your body relax. Drop a clear quartz crystal and a smoky quartz crystal into the water. Sit back and soak for at least 10 minutes. Keep your eyes closed, repeating the affirmation the whole time. Remove the crystals from the water and let it drain out. Stay in the tub until all the water is gone. Cleanse the crystals afterward, before leaving the tub.

With selenite, you can boost the cleansing effects of your meditation practice. Hold the selenite in your non-dominant hand or place it on your crown chakra. Place another piece on the root chakra so that the energy can run through all of your chakras, cleansing them as it goes.

To cleanse your aura, use bloodstone. Hold the crystal in your non-dominant hand and close your eyes. Visualize the energy in the form of white light emanating from the stone and flowing into your body and then allow it to spread outwards until it consumes your aura.

Communication

It is important to be able to communicate effectively. It is an essential ingredient in any healthy relationship. Good communication skills can boost your career, cement your marriage, and help forge lasting bonds that will stick with you for the rest of your life. Your throat chakra is the energy source that powers your communication ability. If you are struggling with poor communication skills, then using meditation and crystals can help you to change.

Affirmation: *I can speak the truth both clearly and calmly*

Meditation: One of the most effective crystals used for communication is the amethyst. It works with the crown chakra to guide and inspire you in your words and how you deliver them. The lapis lazuli works well with your throat chakra, enabling you to be able to speak clearly.

While meditating, sit in a comfortable position with your eyes closed. Place the amethyst on your crown chakra and a lapis lazuli over your throat chakra. Repeat the affirmation for at least ten minutes or until you no longer feel the need to.

Crystals

Other crystals that work well with your communication skills are the rose quartz and sodalite. These work well when you're seeking to improve communication in a personal relationship. Lie on your back and hold a rose quartz over your heart chakra. Place a sodalite stone on your throat chakra. Close your eyes and repeat the chant, "I communicate with love" for ten minutes.

Aquamarine is the best crystal for when you are out and about. It comes in handy whenever you are in a situation where your communication is important. If you wear it as a pendant around your neck or in some form of jewelry, it will always be there, so you can access its energy anytime you need it. Use it on job interviews, or whenever you must have an important conversation with someone.

Keep in mind that communication is not just about knowing what you have to say. A good communicator is also a good listener. If you rearrange the letters in the word listen, you can get the word silent as well. Crystals can help you to know when to be silent and let the other person speak. It will help you to avoid any miscommunication that could lead you down a negative path.

Compassion

Compassion is a powerful emotion that springs from the heart chakra. With compassion, you are able to show deep feelings for others, demonstrate kindness and offer assistance when it is needed. Sometimes it may be difficult to show compassion, especially when it is needed by those close to you. However, the benefits of healing can definitely be enhanced if you know how to show a little compassion in your life.

Affirmation: *The energy of the Divine God lives within me and I recognize its power*

Meditation:

- Find a comfortable place to sit
- Sit with your eyes closed
- Visualize the person that you want to show compassion to
- Repeat the affirmation
- See the white light emanating from your heart
- Watch as it enters the heart of the other person
- Allow the light to envelop both of you completely
- Continue to do this for a minimum of ten minutes

Crystals: Rose quartz works well with your heart chakra. Hold a piece in your non-dominant hand while pressing lightly against your heart chakra. Position your other hand out in front of you with your palm facing up. Close your eyes and visualize the energy emanating from the crystal and filling up your heart chakra. Let it flow out from your dominant hand and spread out into the universe until it finds the person you want to share your compassion with. Continue this meditation for at least ten minutes.

You can also use celestite when you need compassion in a relationship. Carry a small piece of it around with you when you are planning to spend time with anyone you are involved with. It will help you to develop more compassion for that person.

Confusion

We can easily slip into emotional, mental, or spiritual confusion from time to time. Sometimes, it is the result of a physical incident, and other times, it stems from some psychological impact we might have encountered. Whatever the source, confusion can prevent you from growing and progressing as a person. When that happens, you need to find clarity to counteract the chaotic energy caused by the confusion. This will free you up so that you can get back on track with your life and become more productive.

Affirmation: *I can see my life and the choices I've made clearly and can now move forward with self-confidence*

Meditation: To break free from confusion, you need to receive direction from the higher spiritual powers. Only then can you bring about the kind of clarity that will clear away the fog.

- Find a nice, comfortable place to sit
- Close your eyes and breathe normally
- Visualize the pure white light of clarity floating above your crown chakra
- Observe as the light enters your body through the crown and drifts down to the third eye
- Focus on the third eye
- Repeat the affirmation for at least ten minutes or until your confusion fades

Crystals: Ametrine is very effective in clearing away confusion. It works along with the third eye giving you more insight into any situation. It also can be used with your solar plexus, infusing you with more confidence. Carry it around with you wherever you go and when you start to sense the confusion begin to set in, hold it in your hand and with eyes closed, repeat the affirmation ten times or until you start to feel the confusion fade away.

Selenite crystals have a very high-frequency vibration, which can be used to connect you to the wisdom of a higher power. If you are feeling confused, find a quiet place to sit for a few minutes, hold a piece of it in your hand with your eyes closed. Take a few deep breaths and repeat the affirmation. It will help to clear your head and relieve you of the stress that may be causing your confusion.

Contentment

It is not always easy to find contentment in life. It is a feeling you only get when you are happy and at peace with your own personal circumstances. Being content is not a matter of the life you lead, but rather it's a conscious choice to be at peace with whatever situation you are in. So it can be achieved even if you're living a life of distress and chaos.

Affirmation: *I am content and at peace in all circumstances*

Meditation: One way to experience true contentment is to visualize it first through meditation. Your mind might conjure up all sorts of images that trigger the feeling of contentment, a blade of grass yielding to a soft breeze. The kind that will bend but will not break when it is faced with the pressures of the wind. When the wind abates, it will go back to standing upright, facing the sun.

To create these visual images, meditation is often necessary.

- Find a quiet place to sit
- Breathe normally
- Repeat the affirmation as you visualize your image of contentment
- See the blade of grass bending but not breaking
- Watch as it stands tall again in your mind's eye
- Continue with this visualization exercise for at least ten minutes

Crystals: You can enhance your visualization exercises by adding crystals to it. The amethyst is a stone that can be used for a wide range of purposes. Wear it as jewelry or carry it around with you. Hold it in your hand while you visualize the imagery that will instill contentment into your life.

Green aventurine works with your heart chakra, can give you a solid piece of tranquility.

- Lie on the floor and hold the green aventurine on your heart chakra
- Close your eyes and repeat the mantra for at least 10 minutes

You can also use rose quartz, the crystal of unconditional love. Carry a piece of it around with you so you can have it whenever you need it. Keep one in a nearby location so that you can touch it whenever you need to find solace in a particular situation.

Creativity

We are naturally creative beings. This quality exists in all of us and it is passed down from one generation to the next without effort. However, in today's world where creativity is not highly valued, we can seem to lose connection with our own intuitive creative talents. When creativity is lost, it is usually because of a blockage in our sacral chakra. Learning to meditate with crystals can help us to reconnect with this inner quality buried deep inside of us.

Affirmation: *I thank the universe for the unlimited supply of creativity it has given me*

Meditation:

- Find a quiet place to sit comfortably
- Hold a carnelian crystal in your hands
- Close your eyes
- Focus all of your attention on the sacral chakra
- Take a deep inhale
- Visualize your creativity as it flows in from the universe and enters your sacral chakra
- Exhale and feel the creativity flow out of your sacral chakra and spread throughout your entire body
- Continue breathing normally
- As you breathe through this exercise, repeat the affirmation 10 times or to the point where you feel an inner sense of peace and calm.

Crystals: One crystal that taps into creativity quite well is ametrine. It is actually a blend of two different crystals together – the amethyst and citrine. In order to stimulate more creativity in your life, tape the ametrine to the bottom of your chair or place it under your pillow while you sleep.

Water sapphire, another creativity booster, can stir up more inspiration. Wear it as a piece of jewelry or carry it around with you whenever you feel you're going to need a little more inspiration in your life.

If you are a person that makes a living from your creativity, place a bowl of these beads on your desk. They can work to stir up your creative juices throughout the day, keeping your spirit open to receive new and fresh ideas.

As you can see, the list of crystals and the problems they can solve can be quite extensive. We are unable to include all of them within the confines of this book. However, it is clear that you can resolve many of these common problems that all of us have with crystals. In the following chapter, we'll list some of the basic properties of many crystals and give you a general idea of how to use them.

Learning about crystals can require a lifetime of study, but this book and the crystals listed in them is a good place to start. From there, you can research them in more detail on your own.

CHAPTER 10
What Crystal For What?

In this chapter, we'll discuss some of the most commonly used crystals and give you enough information about them, so they will be familiar enough to use them on your own. Each listing will include the crystal origin, its color, and its primary uses. In addition, we'll include which chakras it is best associated with if you plan to use it when working with other crystals, on a grid, or some other form of meditation practice.

Agate

A translucent blend of quartz and chalcedony. It comes in a variety of colors and shapes including round, polished, rough, and slabs. Many agates you find in shops have been dyed to deepen the color in order to enhance its characteristics.

Naturally found in regions of Australia, Brazil, the Czech Republic, India, Mexico, Morocco, and parts of the United States.

Colors: Black, blue, brown, gray, pink, purple, red, yellow, and white
Uses: Emotional balance, yin and yang, calmness, self-confidence, enhance focus and concentration, and heals resentment and bitterness
Chakra: Heart and root
Placement: Place on top of the chakra, hold it in hands, wear as jewelry, carry with you

Blue Lace Agate

Has distinctive gray and white veins running through it. This hard crystal has a light translucent quality and a very polished shine.

Naturally found in parts of South Africa, Australia, and Brazil

Colors: Sky blue, violet-blue with white and gray veins

Uses: Calmness, truthfulness, aids in public speaking, tranquility, reduces deep negative emotions, and assists in communication with spiritual beings.
Chakra: Third eye and throat
Placement: Place the stone on the chakra, hold in your non-dominant hand when seeking calmness, hold in your dominant hand when you need to speak honestly, wear as jewelry, carry with you, or place on a lectern when speaking in public. You can also place it around any room you regularly meditate in.

Moss Agate

This stone is usually the color of moss. The translucent color can vary from a very faint green to a deep green. It has flecks of black, brown, gray, and white.

Naturally found in Australia, Brazil, Czech Republic, India, Mexico, Morocco, and the United States

Color: Green
Uses: encourages appreciation of nature, enhances gardening skills, new beginnings, prosperity, and love for everyone.
Chakra: Heart
Placement: Place on the heart chakra, hold in hands, carry with you, place in your garden

Alexandrite

The color of the Alexandrite can range from a bluish green to a green or a purple. The color will change depending on how it is positioned or how the light hits it. It is a very rare stone and is highly desirable. Most alexandrite you find today is synthetically made from Austrian crystals, which have no healing properties.

Naturally found in Brazil, Russia, and Sri Lanka

Colors: Green to bluish green changing to a deep purple or a raspberry

Uses: Improves self-esteem, deepens positive emotions, promotes confidence, optimism, joy, and luck. It also aids in improved intuition and in a stronger connection with the inner person.
Chakra: heart, third eye, crown
Placement: Place over the chakra, wear it as jewelry, hold in your non-dominant hand, or carry it with you.

Amazonite

From the feldspar family, amazonite sports a range of blue-green and turquoise colors. It has a slight iridescent luster and is relatively soft for a stone. Because of its soft texture, it can be scratched or suffer from dings. It is best to carry it in a protective cloth wrapping to preserve its surface. Never use water or salt to clean this crystal as it could cause permanent damage.

Naturally found in Australia, Brazil, Canada, Namibia, Russia, the United States, and Zimbabwe

Colors: Green and aqua
Uses: Protection from electromagnetic waves, calms and soothes, encourages peacefulness, stress reliever, balances the yin and yang, opens the heart, and embraces love. It also enhances your intuition.
Chakra: heart and throat
Placement: Place on the chakra, use with the third eye for intuition, hold in non-dominant hand for peace, hold in dominant hand for stress, carry it with you or wear as jewelry.

Amber

Technically not a crystal but a fossilized tree resin. It can be found in many places around the world, but the best amber is located in the Baltic region. It has many small impurities like bubbles, small pieces of matter, and even insects that have been trapped inside. Never clean amber with water or salt to prevent damaging its delicate exterior.

Located in the Dominican Republic, Germany, Great Britain, Italy, Poland, Romania, and Russia

Colors: Golden yellow, deep honey brown
Uses: Pain reliever, erase negativity, cleanses auras and chakras, cleanses negative energy from your surroundings, boosts memory, fosters peace, and encourages trust.
Chakra: Solar plexus and throat
Placement: Wear as jewelry, carry it with you, hold in non-dominant hand to attract positive energy

Amethyst

A form of quartz crystal, amethyst can be used for a wide variety of things.

Naturally found in countries like Brazil, Canada, East Africa, Great Britain, India, Mexico, Russia, Sri Lanka, and the United States

Colors: Purple
Uses: Intuition and spiritual insight, aids with sobriety, and heals insomnia. It encourages a restful sleep and enhances psychic abilities, connects to the spirit realm, and to your inner spiritual self.
Chakra: Third eye and the crown
Placement: Place directly on the chakra, wear as jewelry, carry with you, hold in non-dominant hand for receiving, place underneath the pillow when sleeping, or leave it in your meditation room.

Bloodstone

Often used to purify the blood and help heal blood disorders. It is usually green with small red flecks interspersed throughout.

Naturally found in places like Australia, Brazil, China, India, and Russia

Colors: Green with red spots
Uses: Aids in grounding, opens up the heart, and encourages developing a stronger personal power, boosts courage, aids in breaking free from fear, and gives you a stronger strength of mind.
Chakra: Root and heart

Placement: Place directly on the chakra, hold in non-dominant hand for more courage, hold in dominant hand for fear, carry with you, wear as jewelry.

Carnelian

This translucent stone can range in color from a pale orange to a deeper orange-red with inclusions of brown, white, or yellow inside. The spiderweb carnelian has many threadlike bands of white running all the way through it.

Naturally found in areas of the Czech Republic, Great Britain, Iceland, India, Peru, and Romania

Colors: Orange, Brownish orange, and red-orange
Uses: Security and safety, courage, energy, willpower, determination, overcoming abuse, and increased vitality.
Chakra: Root and sacral
Placement: Place directly on the chakra, carry with you, wear it in a small pouch tied around your waist, place next to your bed, keep in the refrigerator or in cupboards.

Desert Rose

This is actually a gypsum stone that can be found in a sandy color with little bands of white. It is rounded with multilayered petals, so it is sometimes referred to as a selenite rose. Because it is primarily made of gypsum, it can be very soft or brittle. Never use water or salt to cleanse it as it can be easily damaged.

Naturally found in places like Austria, France, Germany, Great Britain, Greece, Poland, Russia, and in parts of the United States

Colors: Sandy with white
Uses: Communication with higher beings, focusing the mind, acceptance, calmness, comfort, and cleaning out negative energy.
Chakra: Third eye and the crown
Placement: Place directly on the chakra or hold in your hand during meditation. You can also place pieces of it around your meditation area.

Emerald

This familiar bright green stone is transparent and translucent. In its natural state, it can be found with a rough surface or as a cloudy crystal.

Normally found in countries like Austria, Brazil, Egypt, India, Tanzania, and Zimbabwe

Colors: Green
Uses: Success in romance, faithfulness, unity in relationships, positivity, releasing negativity, and for receiving more wisdom.
Chakra: Heart
Placement: Place directly on top of the chakra, wear as jewelry, or carry with you

Fuchsite

This beautiful green stone has a rough exterior with a slight sparkle when it catches the light. When polished, the color can range from a soft light green all the way up to a deep green with tiny bits of rub inside.

Normally found in places like Brazil, India, and Russia

Colors: Light to very dark green
Uses: Used for enhanced intuition, resolving power struggles, better understanding, feelings of self-worth
Chakra: Heart
Placement: Place directly on the chakra, hold in non-dominant hand when seeking medical intuition, carry with you, wear as jewelry, place in your meditation space, or in a sickroom next to the bed or under a pillow.

Garnet

Garnets come in a wide range of colors, but the most popular choice is red. These help with safety issues and give you a sense of security. Green garnets are used primarily for prosperity and love. Yellow and gold ones boost your self-esteem. Orange garnets help to strength your self-identity and find your place within a particular group.

This crystal has a transparent and translucent appearance and can be distinguished by its deep rich colors.

Garnets are found in almost every place on the planet

Colors: brown, gold, green, orange, red, and yellow
Uses: Cleanses chakras, grounding, promotes passion and love, cleanses negative energies, and can be used to boost the energies emanating from other crystals.
Placement: Place directly on the chakra for cleansing, hold in hands, wear as jewelry, and you can keep it in your meditation area.

Howlite

This beautiful white stone has black bands that sometimes are dyed to a deep turquoise. It is often used as a less expensive alternative for turquoise or lapis lazuli. If you are shopping for either of those two stones, make sure it's not howlite dyed to look like one of them because the properties and characteristics of howlite are very different.

Howlite is only found in the regions of the United States

Colors: White
Uses: Connects to a higher consciousness, balances chakras, insomnia, and patience.
Chakra: Crown
Placement: Place the stone directly on the crown chakra, hold in hands, keep under your pillow or on a night table, or keep in your meditation room

Iron Pyrite

Sometimes referred to as Fool's gold because of its gold-like appearance. Iron Pyrite does not hold the same value as true gold, but you will find soft gold flecks embedded inside the darker stone. It has an opaque quality with a beautiful shiny golden luster.

Normally located in Canada, Chile, Great Britain, Peru, and the United States.

Colors: Gold
Uses: Success in business, prosperity, good fortune, and willpower
Chakra: Solar Plexus
Placement: Place directly on the chakra, carry with you, use in a prosperity corner of the house, place where you keep your cash, keep on your desk at work.

Jade

While jade is most often found in a watery green color, it can also be found in black, purple, red, and white. It is commonly used to improve relationships, help in a decision-making process, and aid in the discovery of inner peace. Its texture is smooth and translucent with a creamy essence to it. Never use water or salt to cleanse jade as it could damage it beyond repair.

Normally Jade is found in certain regions in China, Italy, the Middle East, Russia, and the United States

Colors: Black, green, orange, purple, and white
Uses: Good luck, peace, self-definition, self-knowledge, insight, and guidance
Chakra: works well with all chakras depending on the color you use
Placement: Place directly on the chakra, wear as jewelry, carry with you, hold in hands during meditation, or keep in a meditation room.

Kyanite

This is a silicate mineral with veins of white or gray running through it. It has a rough texture and looks more like a long slab with blades. Polished kyanite is smooth and has a soft luster with swirling bands of white and/or gray. It can be transparent or opaque. Do not cleanse with water or salt so you can preserve its delicate appearance.

Kyanite can only be found in remote regions of Brazil.

Color: Green
Uses: Release negative energy, balance, alignment with all chakras, comprehension, and discernment
Chakra: Heart and the third eye
Placement: Place directly on the chakra, wear as jewelry, carry with you, place in an area that needs to be energized or cleansed.

Lodestone

This naturally magnetic stone is made from black iron oxide. When you examine it, you will notice tiny pieces of magnetic materials that have been attracted to it, giving it a bit of a fuzzy appearance. Always keep your lodestone in a plastic container to keep from drawing in the smaller metal bits. You'll find it is extremely heavy for a stone of its size.

Normally, Lodestone is found in regions of Austria, Central America, Finland, India, Italy, and North America

Colors: Black
Uses: Grounding, to align chakras, and magnify the Law of Attraction
Chakra: Root
Placement: Place near the chakra, carry it with you, or hold it in your hands

Muscovite

Formed from mica, this stone has unique formations that appear to be similar to flakes of slabs from a larger stone. It has a pearlescent and multicolor luster. It holds the same type of energy across all colors of muscovite crystals. It can be very brittle, so always take special care when using or storing it. Never use water or salt to cleanse it because it can erode very quickly.

Normally found in remote regions of Austria, Brazil, Czech Republic, Russia, Switzerland, and the United States

Colors: Gray, green, pink, gold and red
Uses: Connection to higher beings, connections to inner self, guidance and insight, and intuition
Chakra: Third eye and the crown
Placement: Place directly on the chakra, hold gently in hands, keep in meditation area, or put next to your bed for guidance while dreaming.

Obsidian

Obsidian is made from volcanic glass. This lustrous stone can be either smooth or have rough, craggy edges. It comes in a number of different colors, but the most demanded color is black.

It is found in many places around the earth.

Colors: Black, black and white, blue, green, and red
Uses: Grounding, clearing the root chakra, absorbs negativity, coping with grief, strength and energy, emotional protection, and spiritual connections.
Chakra: Root and heart
Placement: Place directly on the chakra, hold in hands, carry with you, place in a room to absorb negative energy, keep a meditation area calm and peaceful.

Peridot

This clear stone comes in varying shades of green. Some will have small black or brown flecks inside. You will often find it cut and polished and used as jewelry.

Normally found in remote areas of Brazil, the Canary Islands, Egypt, Ireland, Russia, and Sri Lanka

Colors: Varying shades of green from a light olive color to a bright apple green
Uses: Opens up the heart chakra, love, emotional trauma, understanding of relationships, protection, cleanses all of your energies (auras, chakras, and meridians).
Chakra: Heart and solar plexus
Placement: Place directly on the chakra, wear as jewelry, carry with you, hold in non-dominant hand, keep in your meditation room. Keep this stone close to you when you are working to build or repair a relationship.

Quartz

Quartz comes in several different colors: clear, rose, rutilated, and smoky. The clear quartz is usually transparent and/or translucent. It is usually found in clusters, geodes, points, or double terminated points. You can buy either polished or rough quartz. The vibration of quartz is quite high and because of this, it is often called upon as a master healer because it can work on almost any condition.

Quartz can be found in every part of the world.

Colors: the clear quartz can be clear or milky white, the rose is a pink color, rutilated can be either clear or smoky with long brown or reddish strands running through it. The term rutilated means that it has fine little needles of titanium dioxide running through it. Smoky quartz has a beautiful brown smoky color.
Uses: Used by shamans in their work, enhances psychic energy, aids in connecting with higher spiritual beings, builds trust in a higher power, cleanses and detoxes energies. It can amplify energy, clean spaces of negative energy, a master healer, cleanses and charges other crystals, and provide protection.
Chakra: Works on all chakras depending on the color. Rose – the root and the heart, rutilated and smoky – solar plexus and the crown. The clear quartz will work with all chakras, especially the crown.

Placement: Place directly on the chakra, carry with you, wear as jewelry, hold in hands during meditation, keep in the meditation area

Rhodochrosite

This beautiful pink stone is banded with white or black strands throughout. It is partially translucent and very soft, so you should always exercise care when using it. Avoid using water or salt with this crystal as it can be damaged.

Normally found in the regions of Argentina, Russia, South Africa, the United States, and Uruguay

Colors: Varying from a light pink to a deeper orange-pink
Uses: Unconditional love, heals a broken heart, resolves emotional issues, love, self-worth, and helps you to forget past hurts
Chakra: Root and heart
Placement: Place directly on the chakra, carry with you, can be placed on any area of the body where your emotional pain is affecting you physically

Sodalite

Very similar in appearance to the lapis lazuli but with a much lighter color. Sodalite usually appears in a denim blue shade with black and/or white spots.

Normally found in the countries of Brazil, Canada, France, Greenland, Myanmar, Romania, Russia, and the United States.

Color: Blue
Uses: Truth and integrity, better communication, intuition, and enhances psychic abilities
Chakra: Throat and third eye
Placement: Place directly on the chakra, hold in the non-dominant hand, wear as jewelry, or keep it in your workspace to enhance creativity

Topaz

This transparent blue (or sometimes yellow) crystal has many facets. It is often used as jewelry even by those who are not into crystal healing. When it has been cut and polished, it is very clear. It can be cut to an extremely small size. The blue topaz helps with communication whether it is internal connections with your inner being, external connections with others, or connecting to a higher being. The yellow topaz enhances self-esteem and guides you in setting boundaries.

Normally found in the countries of Africa, Australia, India, Mexico, Pakistan, and the United States

Colors: Blue or yellow
Uses: Forgiveness, truth and integrity, enhanced communication, fine-tuning thoughts, recharge your energy, empathy, abundance, and joy.
Chakra: Third eye, throat (blue), solar plexus (yellow)
Placement: Place directly on the chakra, wear it as jewelry, carry with you, or keep in your meditation room.

Unakite

This mossy green stone has large spots of pink and peach dispersed through it. You can even see tiny flecks of gold embedded inside. It is a unique type of jasper and can be found either rough, tumbled, or polished.

Mostly found in remote regions of South Africa and the United States.

Uses: Emotional balance, for better sleep, addictions, and boosts willpower
Chakra: Solar plexus and heart
Placement: Place directly on chakras, keep underneath your pillow, on a night table, hold in hands during meditation, or carry with you.

Vanadinite

This stone is formed by the oxidation of mineral ore that contains lead. It can be a yellow, orange, or red color with clear crystals seen in boxy clusters. These stones are usually very small and transparent.

Usually found in regions of Morocco and the United States

Colors: Orange, red, yellow
Uses: Creativity, motivation, mental stimulation, energizing, and moves to action
Chakra: Sacral
Placement: Place directly on the chakra, tape to the bottom of a chair, place in the workspace, under mattress or pillow, on the night table.

Zircon

This stone is often confused with the cubic zirconium. However, zircon is a naturally occurring mineral while the cubic zirconia is purely synthetic. Zircon has many metaphysical properties and can come in a number of different colors including blue, brown, clear, red, or yellow.

It is usually found in countries like Australia, Cambodia, Canada, the Middle East, Myanmar, Sri Lanka, and Tanzania

Colors: Blue and yellow. Comes in other colors but the other colors are usually the result of heat treating.
Uses: Self-love, spiritual growth, communication, amplifies energy from a higher being, aids in intuition.
Chakra: Crown, third eye, throat
Placement: Place directly on the chakra, use while meditating, keep in meditation space, wear as jewelry, carry with you

There is no space or time to list all of the crystals that are available to you. No doubt there are thousands to choose from, but we have just worked to give you a little taste of what's in store. In time, your knowledge of crystals will continue to grow, but for now, it is important to start experimenting with the ones listed here. Soon, you'll be ready to venture out into a broader landscape and put all of your newfound knowledge to the test.

CONCLUSION

Now that you have found a better understanding of crystals and the many ways you can use them, you are probably anxious to get started. It is amazing to learn just how these beautiful little gems will affect the body and the mind.

Don't worry too much about getting all the details right. There are a lot of them, and for a time, you'll have to refer back to these pages for clarification. Intuitively, you already know what to do, just learn how to trust yourself. Your mind is a creation from the Divine God of the universe and He wants you to be pulled towards him.

This is the point where most people start their journey, how about you? I promise you, it will be a ride to be remembered, no matter what happens.

Hopefully, you found this information both informative and humbling. It is amazing how many secrets are hidden within arm's reach. Once you tap into all that energy floating around there, you'll be well on your way to a future of wonders.

DESCRIPTION

Anyone ready to make some serious changes in their lives, this book is for you. When life throws us lemons, we can fight back with crystals. Learn how to reclaim your life with the power of these beautiful gems.

Whether you're just trying to get your feet firmly planted on the ground, or you're dealing with deeper psychological challenges, you'll get the basics for beginners who wish to explore the world of crystals. Here in these pages, you'll learn...

- What exactly are crystals
- How to tap into crystal energy
- You and your chakras
- How to make a crystal grid
- The fundamentals of healing with crystals
- Tips on finding the right crystals for you
- And much, much more.

You'll learn basic properties of crystals and how to take advantage of them, and be all the better for it.

If you're looking for another way to fulfill your life, then this is the book you've been searching for. If you listen closely, you might even hear it calling to you. So, why not answer it and download this book today.

www.ingramcontent.com/pod-product-compliance
Lightning Source LLC
Chambersburg PA
CBHW071501070526
44578CB00001B/408